DENIS DEVLIN
COLLECTED POEMS

DENIS DEVLIN

COLLECTED
POEMS

Edited and with an Introduction by
BRIAN COFFEY

THE DOLMEN PRESS

*Printed at the Monument Press, Bray, for the
Dolmen Press Limited, 23 Upper Mount Street, Dublin 2, in
the Republic of Ireland.*

*

*First published as a special number
of University Review, Dublin 1963*

First published in book form 1964

*Distributed outside Ireland by
Oxford University Press*

ACKNOWLEDGEMENTS

Grateful thanks are made here to *The Arts Council* for a grant which made the publication of the *University Review* edition possible.

To the Contessa Marie Caren di Gropello, widow of Denis Devlin, for her encouragement and help at every stage in the preparation of this volume,

To Mervyn Wall, Secretary of *The Arts Council*, for his wise and friendly advice,

To Moya Lindsay, sister of Denis Devlin, for answering many questions of fact about her brother,

To Niall Montgomery, for information about the franco-gaelic translations referred to in the *Notes* to this volume,

To Agnes Raw, who worked against time to type a long and difficult manuscript,

The Editor of *Poems of Denis Devlin* wishes to record here his grateful thanks.

The volume *Lough Derg and Other Poems*, incorporated in the present book, carried the dedication: TO ADRIENNE.

Acknowledgement of the first publication of some of the poems printed in this book: *Memoirs of a Turkoman Diplomat* (Botteghe Oscure, 1959); *The Passion of Christ* (Encounter, 1957); *Mr. Allen* (The Irish Times, 1958); *The Collours of Love* (Botteghe Oscure, 1952); *The Heavenly Foreigner* (Poetry Ireland, 1950).

Some of the poems in *Lough Derg and Other Poems* appeared in: The Dublin Magazine, Ireland To-day, Transition, Calendar, The Southern Review, The New Republic, The Irish Times, The Maryland Quarterly, The University Review, The Briarcliff Quarterly, Poetry, Accent.

Now, among the *First Poems*, appeared in The National Student.

The poems published posthumously all appeared first in the *Selected Poems by* Denis Devlin, published by Holt, Rinehart & Winston, New York, in 1963.

CONTENTS

INTRODUCTION by Brian Coffey   *page* xi

NOTES   xv

Addendum: The Investiture of d'Artagnan   xxiii

I PUBLISHED POEMS

Memoirs of a Turcoman Diplomat	3
Mr. Allen	7
The Passion of Christ	8
The Tomb of Michael Collins	15
The Colours of Love	17
The Heavenly Foreigner	21

II LOUGH DERG AND OTHER POEMS (1946)

Lough Derg	35
Encounter	38
From Government Buildings	38
The Statue and the Perturbed Burghers	39
Memo from a Millionaire	40
Royal Canal	42
Mixed Drinks	42
Jansenist Journey	43
West Pier	45
Est Prodest	46
Handy Andy	50

Ballad of Mistress Death   50
On Mount Muckish   52
Meditation at Avila   53
Old Jacobin   56
Anteroom: Geneva   57
Argument with Justice   58
Pays Conquis   59
Boy Bathing   60
Bacchanal   60
After Five O'Clock   64
Annapolis   64
Tantalus   66
The Blind Leading the Blind   66
Freedom No Object   67
Celibate Recusant   67
Obstacle Basilisk   68
Daphne Stillorgan   69
Welcome My World   70
Summer Jujube   72
Poet and Comic Muse   73
Victory of Samothrace   74
The Lancet   76
Venus of the Salty Shell   77
Edinburgh Tale   78
Between the Late and Early   79
Eve in my Legend   80
Wishes for Her   81
Little Elegy   82
Picture in a Window   83

Farewell and Good   85
Love from Time to Time   86
A Dream of Orpheus   87
Vestiges   89
Lakeside   90

III INTERCESSIONS (1937)

The Alembic   93
Death and Her Beasts, Ignoble Beasts   93
Windtacker Windjamming   94
Liffey Bridge   95
Gradual   97
In the Last Resort   98
Communication from the Eiffel Tower   98
Entry of Multitudes into an Eternal Mansion   106

IV FIRST POEMS (1930)

O Paltry Melancholy   111
Before Lepanto: The Turkish Admiral
Speaks to His Fleet   112
Adam's House   113
Now   116

V POEMS PUBLISHED POSTHUMOUSLY (1963)

Jealousy   121
Aztec Idol   121
Val D'Aosta   122

Mother Superior in the City of Mexico 122

Abel 124

VI UNPUBLISHED POEMS

Hobby-Horses 127

Piccadilly Centre 127

By the Boat Train 127

Poem 128

Tiger-Emperor 129

Good-Bye and Good Luck 129

Boyhood 130

Renewal by Her Element 131

INTRODUCTION

Bíonn a shlighe féin ag gach file
Agus a chaint féin ag gach bard
Ní lia tír ná gnás
A's ní lia ceann ná céard.

A way of his own has every poet
And every bard his own way finds;
So many lands, so many habits,
So many heads, so many minds.

(Dr. Douglas Hyde)

It is difficult, if not altogether valueless, to try to fit poets into a scheme of classification, poets being as it were, each one an individual *infirma species*.

It was peculiar to Denis Devlin (1) that while Nature did not stir him to poetry, places did (2). He recorded his dreams through a long period of his life, forcing them to yield a poetry, yet he rejected the automatic techniques of surrealism (3).He was dependent, as much as any poet, on an inspiration, which does not imply that he did not approach the task of verse-making in a conscious and wholly deliberate manner (4). He sought to relate his intelligence and his memory to the traditions of his race and at the same time he sought the fertilising effect upon himself of foreign poetries (5).

Usually one does not find the theme of Love and Death (6) and the theme of Justice (7) associated in a poet's practice, as they were in the poetry of Denis Devlin. One might have thought that a poet who was interested in Justice:

.... with any and every language armed
To strike them down, the company of the evil heart:
would
have worked with a group or in a movement. For Denis Devlin that kind of participation was not proper for a poet. It is asked: where was he going, what might he have done had he lived? The answer to that question: *whither?* in

respect of Denis Devlin will be found, I believe, in the answer to the other question: *whence?*

He grew up in a happy home. Of his parents, indeed, what could be said enough? The home to which he invited one, during student days, was a place in which, to use a phrase of which my own father was fond, "learning and manners make charming companions". Eldest and beloved son, the roots of family and home fed the life of the grown man:

At last we reached the Gospel gates,

Aching and dirty. Robes lay there.
Mother and sisters like light through glass,
With stopped lightning stood in the arch.

(Jansenist Journey)

He intended the priesthood, on leaving school, and he entered the seminary with a mind filled with the imaginative literatures of England and France, already exercised in poetic vision. Though well endowed for voluntary activity and moral analysis, he did not, I believe, take either to logical studies or professionalism. The experience of seminary life left indelible marks in him; I, for one, always associated with the seminary that mass of reserve of his, which struck so many people as noteworthy. He spoke rarely, and with discretion, of that period of his life; its traces, in his poetry, come to the surface most obviously, I believe, in *The Heavenly Foreigner,* in which this poet, with his catholic conscience (a distinguishing feature of his from poets in the English tradition) schooled in the great book of European learning, faces the personal struggle of a soul (sealed Christ's in Christ's Church) which is at once enchanted by the voice of Christ and by the voice of a love which stands for all the the voices of all the creatures of this world, (which are all good): *est bonitas una omnium et multae bonitates.*

Of the abiding influence upon him of the Irish political scene at the time of the Treaty and the response to events, history and literature by a nature sympathetic, passionate and intelligent, no one could speak better than Denis Devlin has done himself in that noble poem, written by one Irishman of another who vivified our boyhood for us all, namely: *The Tomb of Michael Collins.*

Such are the factors which influenced the making of Denis Devlin's poetry in its beginnings. The rest was his life.

There is plenty of evidence in the poems of this volume of

a conflict of ravaging intensity which for many years finds expression only in a love poetry so positive that the opposing pole of the conflict hardly comes clearly into sight. In a poem called *Venus of the Salty Shell* (and which he called *Aisling* in an early manuscript) the poet sees the goddess:

> The smiling idol of love
> Brightness shadowy through brightness
> She smiles as if turning all the orchards of summer
> Into one brittle petal to touch.

And he sees her again (*Picture in a Window*) in verses which echo hauntingly those in which Catullus described the arrival of his *candida dea*:

> Or see in the dark her corndusky hair,
> The breath held in, the foot upon the stair.

In the perfect *Eve in my Legend*, there is an expression of heaven on earth:

> Nothing to know that is not she
> Nor she know anything but me.

But in *Farewell and Good*:

> Whatever I do, unreal, I may find my hand, once hers,
> Bled on the wall in a crack of anger and veins blocked
> And eyes glazed that will break open to hers no more . . .

And in *The Colours of Love*, in verses which, although they were not written out of the tradition of courtly love (of which, like so many of the Gaelic poets, Denis Devlin was well aware), might well sum up the European sentence upon that extraordinary phenomenon: Better no love than love, which, through loving leads to no love: the poet seems to free himself from his conflict in its overt form, and thus, mature, turn inward to the personal life out of which issued *The Passion of Christ*: (8)

> With such certainty ascended He,
> The Son of Man who designed Himself to be:
> Then when we lifted out of sleep, there was
> Life with its dark, and love above the laws.

Denis Devlin did not say much about the nature of poetry. According to a note found among his papers (but unsigned): "The poetic works of x must be the revelation of a single person to the world". That conception of the poetic activity does lie behind the sensuously dense verse of *Intercessions*. Then, later, in an appreciation of the great French poet St. John Perse, he wrote: "The poet, master and keeper of lauguage, that most characteristic discovery of man, that mark by which you will know him..." And last of all, on his death-bed he wrote: "The poet justifies the works of man to God", adding thus a statement which was lacking to the poetic *Sic et Non,* and which is glossed in the first stanza of *The Passion of Christ*: "We fall and rise, God's instrument, and sing".

If I were to attempt the classificatory act I should say that there are poets for whom it is laid down that a great distance separates the initial movement with its inspiration from the last state of the chosen words. Such poets labour to make a form in words which, on account of their sensuous qualities and interrelationships *and* on account of their capacity as signs, make possible the placing or situating of something (which is the poem) analogous to the inital movement *and* make possible secondarily the enjoyment by other persons of that thing. Poets of this kind are usually good translators. Their own work is a kind of translation which (subject to betrayal by a material which is at once words and their own selves) sometimes reaches as near as may be perfection. Poets of that kind are usually called classical; they are driven to seek mastery rather than, as do the romantics, singularity.

It was then the singularity of Denis Devlin that he sought mastery. Man of his own way as he was, he points out a direction to other poets, namely mastery of language at the disposition of one who pursues self-knowledge unrelentingly to the point of freedom from passing fashions, passing avidities, to the point of a true judging of the goods of this world and the next. Mastery of language is one abiding aim of the poet. Denis Devlin became a master of language.

NOTES

DENIS DEVLIN: Born 15th April, 1908, in Greenock, Scotland, of Irish parents.

First formal instruction, in the local school.

The family returned to Ireland when Denis was about twelve years old. His schooling continued, first under the Christian Brothers, later under the Jesuits at Belvedere College, Dublin. On leaving school Denis began training for the priesthood.

In 1926, he was at Clonliffe, and attending courses at University College, with a view to taking a degree in modern languages. In 1927 he left Clonliffe.

1930, B.A. In the summer of this year he went to the Blaskets for the first time, in order to develop his knowledge of Gaelic.

In 1930-31, literary studies at Munich University.

In 1931-33, literary studies at La Sorbonne, Paris.

April, 1932, first visit to Spain, including a visit to Avila.

1933, appointment to an assistantship in the English Department, University College. M.A., with a thesis on Montaigne.

At some time between 1933 and 1936 he made a tour of Cathedral towns in England and Scotland.

In 1935 he entered the Department of External Affairs, as Cadet.

1938, First Secretary, Legation to Italy. First visit to Greece.

1939, Consul, New York Consulate-General.

1940, First Secretary, Legation to Washington.

1946, married Marie Caren Radon. Visited Mexico.

1947, Counsellor, Office of the High Commissioner, London.

1949, Counsellor at Headquarters.

1950, Minister Plenipotentiary to Italy.

1951, accredited to Turkey as Minister Plenipotentiary.

1958, Ambassador to Italy.

1959, August 21st died in Dublin.

1 (b) Note on this edition.

Lough Derg and Other Poems, by Denis Devlin, has long been out of print. Between 1946 and his death in 1959, Denis published only occasionally, nearly always in periodicals, in *Botteghe Oscure* for example, where other poets might find him. During the last year of his life, as I know from a statement in one of his letters to me, he was arranging to publish a new collection of his poems. The projected volume would have included all the poems published between 1946 and 1959, many of the pieces in the *Lough Derg* collection, and a number of new poems of which there exist fragments, in various stages of finish. (In one case, that of a poem entitled *Light in the Country*, the manuscript yielded a text clear enough to admit of publication; the fragment thus recovered appeared in *Poetry Ireland*, March 1964.

For a short while after his death, his widow, his relatives and his friends were hoping for an early publication of all Denis' poems in one volume. A resultant of that friendly concern was the publication, early this year, in New York, of *Selected Poems*. (Holt, Rinehart & Winston Inc.) This carefully made selection contains an introduction by co-editors Allen Tate and Robert Penn Warren; naturally, it will not, because not complete, serve the purposes of the student of poetry. We should all, therefore, be grateful to the Editor of *University Review*, Dr. Lorna Reynolds, for taking the opportunity allowed by existing copyright law in deciding to publish all of Denis' poems in a single issue of the review.

This edition of *Poems of Denis Devlin* contains:
a) *all the poems published by the author during his life-time*. These poems have been arranged in an order which begins with the poem published most recently and ends with the poem of earliest publication, in keeping with the idea of chronological order. The dates of publication of the poems will be found with their titles in the *Table of Contents*. The reason for adopting the order I have described was the desirability of avoiding patterns of private interpretation in presenting an author to readers many of whom will be discovering him for the first time. It has not been possible, given the state of the manuscripts, to date individual poems.

b) *Poems published posthumously*.
c) *A few poems which have not been published before*.

This edition does not include:

a) *published translations*—from St. John Perse (1945-49, *Exile, Rains, Snows*, and *Poem to a Foreign Lady*, published in the United States in several editions), from Paul Eluard (some of the pieces in the Europa Press, London, publication, *Thorns of Thunder*, 1936), from Rene Char (poems: in *Botteghe Oscure*, 1952), from Paul Valéry (Palm, published in Quarterly Review of Literature III, No. 3).

b) *unpublished translations*—A large number of translations from Goethe and Du Bellay (including translations of poems on Rome by these authors, intended by Denis for a book on Rome), plus translations from Verlaine, Laforge, Apollinaire, Quasimodo and others.

c) *unpublished translations from French into Gaelic*—this collection was a joint project involving Denis and his friend Niall Montgomery. There were to be translations of poems by Verlaine, Nerval, Baudelaire, Rimbaud, Mallarmé, Valéry, Gide, Nouveau, Fargue, Larbaud, Cocteau, Appollinaire, Jacob, Reverdy, Cendrars, Souppault. (I follow the list as given in Denis' handwriting.) Denis translated the following items: *Verlaine*: O triste, triste: Il pleut dans mon coeur; Un grand somneil noir— *Nerval*, Les Cydalises—*Baudelaire*: Receuillement—*Rimbaud*: Comédie de la Soif; Bruxelles; Génic; Veillées;

Départs—*Mallarmé*: Brise Marine; *Valéry*: Cimetière Marin; Les Pas—*Fargue*; Kiosques; Nocturnes; Aeternae Memoriae Patris — *Cocteau*: L'Espagne — *Apollinaire*: Zone; Chanson du Mal-Aimé—*Jacob*: Brésil—*Souppault*: Chansons. Some of Montgomery's translations were published in *Ireland Today*. The collection can well be described in the words of Tate and Warren as "one of the curiosities of literature"; of it Professor Liam O'Briain wrote, many years ago, to Niall Montgomery, at the end of a long letter of detailed constructive criticism: "If you have attempted something practically impossible in the present state of Irish, it is at any rate magnificent and tremendously heartening to us old stagers who have too many reasons to be downhearted...if you are really going to publish this at your own expense, for goodness sake don't let anything I have said stop you. And who can say what seed you may sow, and what strange plant may spring from it?"

d) *the fragments of an unfinished prose autobiography*, and other prose pieces.

2 Denis was deeply affected by places. He frequently noted down his first impressions of a place, usually in verse form; a fragment about Acupulca begins:

Down the burnt grass, down the falling hills,
The dust swirled from the road like a dancer's skirt....

Occasionally he noted down his observations of behaviour, achieving an irony by benefit of local presence, as in this short piece entitled: PANAMERICAN:

In the plane the bored steward:
"That's Athens Greece on yr. left;
Below, some units of the Mediterranean fleet".
He muttered off. Also on our left,
The Acropolis could be seen in the tawny sun.
The same cloud-born ignorer
        of all men's misery and grandeur muttered later:
"On yr. right, if you can see
        what looks like a stream,
That's the Dardanelles",

Readers of the poems will notice the constant reference to place. In one case, of a version of *The Heavenly Foreigner* not so far published (and to be published in the near future in a Dolmen Press *variorum* edition of the poem), the movement of the meditation is explicitly associated with passage from place to place, the places being, in this case, cathedrals.

3 The manuscripts include a number of poems bearing the title *Adventure*. It seems that at one stage a volume of *Adventures* was projected. These poems are closely related to dreams which Denis had recorded. *The Blind leading the Blind* grew out of an earlier *Adventure*. So did *Summer Jujube*, and *Jansenist Journey*.

4 All of Denis' literary activity was deliberate, in the sense that he predetermined the form (or at least a form) through which he would pursue the implications of any given inspiration. He once asked me to write a poem accounting for the situation in which a penniless man who is leading a lady of wealth to the grandstand of a racing track decides after all not to propose marriage. His papers contain a long list of "ideas" for sonnets. On reading his poem: *The Tomb of Michael Collins* I queried the line: "It was all sky and heather" as a possible echo of Dylan Thomas. He replied (18-12-57): "The reference to Dylan Thomas is not pertinent—I haven't read him since London, since the beautiful "The child burnt in the air-raid". The popularesco repetitions "It is..." "It was..." come, deliberately, from the Irish ballad, my aim being to make a ceremonial ode with country ballad elements". [His last poems are visibly the perfected forms of his first essays—growth from deliberate continuity.]

5 Passing over the classics of French and English literature which can be taken as read in Denis' case, one notes, however, particularly Racine and Baudelaire in French literature, Chaucer, Shakespeare and Browning in English literature (and, curious fact, he had read all the works of Victor Hugo before he left school). He was aware of the sources of courtly love; there are copies of poems in Provençal among his papers. He had studied Dante, and Petrarch. One can trace the effect of both St. John of

the Cross and St. Teresa on Denis (he had read widely in recent Spanish poetry). I have mentioned elsewhere his study of the classics of Gaelic bardic poetry. German poetry affected him deeply. He was reading German lyrics, with delight, in hospital, shortly before he died. From his conversation I was aware that for him Goethe was one of the great poles of regulation in his approach to poetry. To the influence of Goethe I would trace his tendency to write to occasion. A reviewer of *Lough Derg*, Arthur Mizener, suggested that occasionalness might well be a danger for Denis. It did not subsequently prove so. Two other German influences which went deep were Novalis and Hölderlin.

6 Death is not separable from Love in our world, because the loves we experience exist in the moving instant. Christians would not qualify the departing *spiritus* as *indignatus*, and yet must prepare themselves for noughting in transition. His poems reflect the many times Denis viewed death. Two passages from unfinished poems which might otherwise be lost are here recorded because of what they add to the published material in this respect.

a) a poem in memory of that gentle man and great scholar Gerard Murphy:

If one were purified by Hell like the great florentine
    he loved
Another's death would not be one's selfish own;
And through the misery one would see his gentle smile
of one who has conquered pain and regarded others—
Whether mediaeval Ireland or epical noble expressions
Or us his brash crude students—long ago, long before
    death
With him round the fire, while the sun nearby
And the sea nearby breathed through its green aged
    lungs.

b) verses corrected while he was in hospital before death:

When you think, right, that Death's our enemy
For that he knocks us out; and is our friend
For he defines our quality by its end:

You wish some Master Angel of the sun
Would root us out again, put back the flesh,
And polish it and set us up again.

7 During the thirties many poets included political loyalties
on the active revolutionary level in their notion of themselves as poets. Denis understood political loyalties in
terms of vivid memories of Michael Collins, who realised
for him in the flesh the heroes of history who lived in his
mind, and in terms of family involvement in national
politics. When he became aware of the political poetry of
the thirties, it was not in the way in which Day-Lewis'
young poet required to be initiated into Communism;
already he had formed political views, out of family
history and traditions, out of historical reading, out of
sympathy for his fellows, and out of a deeply felt respect
for human dignity. During the time when he was making
his mind up about the political forces working in the
thirties and simultaneously making poems like, for
example, *Bacchanal*, changes in the character of his reflections were manifested by the frequent changes of titles of
given poems. Titles, for Denis, were important; *Bacchanal*
was at one time entitled *News of Revolution*. At the end,
he had satisfied himself that political solutions are not
sufficient for human happiness.

8 Of *The Passion of Christ* he wrote to me: "I am interested
in its fate. I think I have done a good piece of work".

9 One of the reviewers of *Lough Derg and Other Poems*
caught well the root principle of this intention of mastery. Writing in the *New York Times* (21-7-46),
Marguerite Young noted that Denis' poems were steeped
in many traditions, "highly discursive, tapestries of many
moods, unified not so much by the abstraction of intellectual argument as by the all-encompassing ego which
believes itself to be the unifying principle". What was
left for a poet, writing during the years of levity between
the two wars, when a mind nourished on Montaigne was
ill-prepared for intellectual assertion, when a velleity of
Goethean superiority had come to flesh in the wrong
century, was the cultivation of a *classical temper of will*.
That was, I believe, the quality which, having survived

the years of experimentation and growing self-knowledge, reappeared perfected in the years following marriage to form and ensoul the last and the great poems of Denis' life.

It is worth noting here what is perhaps a trace of the admiration for Goethe to which I have referred, in the Denis of 1933. An unfinished, though many times attempted poem: *Statement of an Irishman*, which underlines the poet's statement, that he does not care for language except as an instrument of justice, has the lines:

Afterwards, complaint stilled, gesture
Will suffice for the little necessary pure expression.

It is Goethean to feel the weakness of language in so far as it is abstract. He says: "We ought to talk less and draw more. I, personally should like to renounce speech altogether and, like organic nature, communicate everything I have to say in sketches". (Quoted in *Encounter*, p. 62, Nov. 1962.)]

ADDENDUM

There exist a number of both manuscript and typescript copies of variant drafts of the poem: The Investiture of d'Artagnan. *No copy was dated; there was no indication that publication in any form had ever taken place nor did any of those of whom I made enquiry remember the publication of such a poem. In those circumstances, I decided not to include my own choice from among the possible versions in the collected poems. Quite by accident, and when it was too late to do anything, I noticed that the poem had been published in* The Dublin Magazine *(July-September, 1936); it is reproduced below.*

THE INVESTITURE OF D'ARTAGNAN

Crimson, diamonds and black eye-brows, trees no rough
    Spring rescinds.
I am still lorded by these red-heeled bucks with bird brains.
My cloak falls indolently as theirs, O my ragged cranes
Reproach me from the shy rectitude of our gray Biscayan
    winds.

With you is my last dignity in retreat from these the precise
    great.
By Clio squandered. I have pacted with the time unworthy
    of my chance,
Embroidered, twisting a feckless baton, first marshal of
    France
Who should have ridden the times in spasm, have been I the
    State.

Bitter to take. Bitter to get all except my will, foiled feeder:
My epoch's weaned too soon. How the Emperor pounded
    provinces cutting through
The obedient mammals that barely tumble above clay and
    spew . . .
Some other age jagged into fear waits to fulfill its leader.

Everything else. Faces light up and eyes when I come near
Bow my burgher, Condé had not such honour, the armies
    so in nature

Personal with me, they love me not like a conscious creature
Rather as the ocean reflects the whim of the sky in
    spontaneous fear

Most men fret for such love whom the saviour lighthouse
    solitude would drive mad:
Such like gummed to like for proof of life: which irks me for
I could mock myself into danger their laws and their
    laundered heart abhor,
A king-pet in lace of minuets woven like the age mends bad

Foreclosed. Not to be captain conqueror of kneaded minds
    is my gift
To resignation, smile to the King, Sire I cannot leave
These lawns the hereditary breezes bevel, this soft life a
    reprieve
From my intended life...Remember on the last mountain
    drift

Of snow in May, the depth, insects and birds cried in birth,
    the breeze
Freshened the streams and as the whole blue sky opened, my
Plumes beat the sun, I swung my cold sword and screeched, I
D'ARTAGNAN flushed among a flurry of eagles in the
    Pyrenees.

I

PUBLISHED POEMS:

MEMOIRS OF A TURCOMAN DIPLOMAT

OTELI ASIA PALAS, INC.

Evenings ever more willing lapse into my world's evening,
Birds, like Imperial emblems, in their thin, abstract singing,
Announce some lofty Majesty whose embassies are not
    understood,
Thrushes' and finches' chords, like the yellow and blue skies
    changing place,
I hold my stick, old-world, the waiters know me,
And sip at my European drink, while sunlight falls,
Like thick Italian silks over the square houses into the
    Bosphorus.
Ladies, I call you women now, from out my emptied
    tenderness,
All dead in the wars, before and after war,
I toast you my adventures with your beauty!
Where the domes of Sinan shiver like ductile violets in the
    rain of light.

To the Franks, I suppose it's ugly, this brick and oblong,
When a rare sunlight, rare birdsong,
Compose the absolute kingdom far in the sky
The Franks must ask how it was known, how reached,
    how governed, how let die?
This woman who passes by, sideways, by your side:
There was one you loved for years and years;
Suddenly the jaw is ugly, the shoulders fall,
Provoking but resentment, hardly tears.

THE GOLDEN HORN

We all have a magic kingdom, some have two,
And cry: "O my city on the Golden Horn, and
    O my you!"
Discover, in the bee flaunting his black and gold among the
    foliage in the frieze,
You are not what you thought, you are someone like all
    these,
The most ardent young man turn, at the drop of a black hat,

3

Into some rabbity sort of clerk, some heart-affairs diplomat,
A John of the Cross into a Curia priest.
It was years ago. It is not now like when the century
    began—
Though apple and peach lie brilliant on the dark,
And mineral worlds on the dark sky shine,
And the red mouth breathes in; thine is mine,
And the careless Atlantic inhales the Thames, the Tagus
    and the Seine,
Murmuring back and murmuring forward beasts and sonata
    scores and Ophelian rags—
Where a girl in her balldress was a light on the wave,
Where a dying flare was like a firefly on the wave,
Where all the waves shivered with phosphorous under the
    moon's glacial withdrawal—
"Me voici ignorant": so a poet my father read.
The Empire born again, old pedants will rake up the dead.

My father thought my feeling could take fire by the vibrant
    Seine
And a tough intellect be constructed in Gottingen,
He thought, the citadels of Anatolia I could justify
Making what's hungry full, what's ragged spry.
Opalescent on the unbloodied green, the Sultan's battle
    horse,
The hungry cavalry, rearing and screaming in the mist:
We put them down, these Franks, in their sweaty leather
    and blasphemous curse,
Our salaried Levantine admirals sank their trading ships.
It happened: the Prophet conquered with murder in his
    hand and honour in his crescent lips.

Put it down to a thick heart and a thick pate,
Such puritanic temperament's outgrown:
Now some international Secretary-General throws a lump
    of bait
And laughs and says my country's not my own.

There was a professor who said: "The horse must go!"
And certain poets praised him to their shame,
Except in County Cork and Mexico
And where the quick darlings to us from the Cossacks came.
In the Foreign Office, they humorously ask my advice,

My father had money, I was posted from place to place:
What can I tell them? even if I got it right?
There would be protocol about the right time and the
    right place,
And even not too sentimental about the corps of horse
Dancing between the up-country captains' harsh knees
They could assert that horses than humanity were worse—

And that our Westernising dictator, though free was no
    longer free
When at Smyrne he tumbled the chatterbox Greeks into
    the sea,
Turk lieutenants, waxed moustaches and all, and spiritless
    mugs of tea.

WARS OF RELIGION

All is when I remember and forget
The Prophet drops the sword and shuts the Book
Down the green wind the Lord came, I met
The Lord, but did not feel or hear or look,

Interrupted by the Exarch shouting, we robbed Greece—
It's true—those comedians with their epics,
Their Aphrodite, their Achilles, their Golden Fleece,
Shouting the Prophet down, with their rational septics,

Even their best, their Hector, did not know,
Or mother Venus with her bog and milk,
Gesso Olympians dancing heel and toe—
Why should a Turk care about that ilk?

FOUR TURKISH WOMEN

The true, the loyal moon, not like her mother,
She was the plasma we assembled to:
All sky flows, water and blood and spittle,
Mother degraded in her human brew.

Moon! rest our emblem...not like Europeans
Whose stupid sun discovers all their dirt.

5

O Crescent, sweet and careless above the water—
Yet infidel fingers hurt

A woman, my Frankish Friend's one wife,
In a far Latin villa held his hand;
It was night all at once, and kind of grief
And kind of laughter, and kind with hand in hand.

ANATOLIA

In the high country, there is no food for ghosts,
The dead stay underground, which is their place
We had enough to do to keep the Arabs and the Bulgars
    in their place
If the dead have bad dreams they live in us, querulous
    and lost.

Must we believe that hatred or freedom, the Sultan Ahmet
    risen on his medieval horse, turns to love?
Fail to regret the Empire, the Franks and the Hohenstaufen?
Europa and the Turk Bull?
The President of the Republic bends this way and that,
A bubble on the corner of his lips,
The Franks have their shopkeeper saints, Saint Thomas
    Aquinas,
(And Saint Thomas putting his hand in the Wound)
How can you think it's sure if you're a coward?

RISTORANT PIK NIK

The trams go tired home in the Istliqal Caddesi,
Rue du Pera, we said—the Frankish end.
The waiter flicks off a crumb. It was lamb and rice;
Would you raise your knife to stick an indifferent friend?

THE TURKISH FOR GREEK IS ROMAN

Why we call the Greeks Romans I know not
Nor without grammar do I care not:
Both were here before we were, but hear not
Nor grudge, nor love nor hate, they're lost and know not.

The Sava and the Danube like two horses folded, mane
   on mane,
And there were dogs which lapped the water up:
Pale sunlight and pale water, as if some great poet
Said there was peace, like Goethe, and there was peace.

The sunlight pressing on the eyelids, on the waters;
Only ten years ago the invaders came,
The pretty guide talked on and showed our party—
In which were former Nazis, former Fascists—
Photo-posters of men hanging like blotting paper,
Dirty blood on dirty children, dirty mothers
The willowy waters of the Sava bathed;
Only three hundred years ago
Sulymein the Magnificent
Sick and sad outside Belgrade.

Who knows his expectations, free or slave?
Join me, Johannes, down this pretty brace:
One said, or could have sung, Come out with me,
The other, A truce to talk of genocide, and nation and race!

Tuck in your trews, Johannes, my boy, be led by me,
These girls are kind. And we're all the rage now,
   whisky-flushed men of our age,
The callow and the sallow and the fallow wiped off
   the page!

MR. ALLEN

From Dreghorn to the Royal and Antient Borough
Of Irvine, Mr. Allen walked my road,
I waited for him while the amber bees
Danced in the window up and down the sunlight,
Old friezecoat teacher with his violin
Under his arm, which in his mind he played:

His red Scots Guard's moustaches turning white,
He played back all his life those seven miles:
His ear was antiquarian, yet he heard

7

All the fledglings fumbling in the hedgerows
Whose song I knew; and all ephemeras, too.

Mr. Allen stamped into the schoolroom
From Tierra del Fuego, worlds away;
In vain seals barked in his unpublished concert—
It was before those mimes, the Elder Persons
Took on their tragic, minatory role....

II

Sad! to his numbered years the avid summer
Firing the hedgerows, sounded Omen! Omen!
But cool and sweet I had the room arranged:
Dark red chrysanthemums, the dead, the dead,
Like the flare above the steelworks of Kilwinning,
Like the ashes in the pipe which he put down,

He put the bow down, too: "Mr. Allen, Mr. Allen,
If it's true we'll never play again together:
It's true your only heaven is in my mind!
Even your cousin ghosts by now have left you ...
What pain, what pride, what persiflage your life!
Teaching Glasgow brats, and then for years
With bronze translated Spaniards in the pampas,
On horseback with your pipe and violin."

THE PASSION OF CHRIST

to Allen Tate

THE FALL
From what did man fall?
From the Archangel Michael's irritated wing?
Man is so small,
Without him first the universe did sing,
So fortunate since the Christ endued his caul:
Let us take on the whole
Story in its negligence and passion—
Archangel, we your images that fall,
Dissolve and reassemble, session by session.
You rise and rise, God's wasp, and sting!
We fall and rise, God's instrument, and sing!

THE GARDEN OF EDEN

Leaving the Garden, our first father stayed
Behind, and wept, and death is still delayed.

THE MAN OF SORROWS

He sought our sorrow out and bought it back
From merchants in the back streets of the heart:
But we, suspended between love and lack,
    Will neither sign off nor take part.

THE ANNUNCIATION

What we have best imagined is the Mother
Who, with the absolute, say Light, brought forth
Self, without intervention of the Other,
    The pure, the Virgin birth.

Gabriel, death-borne on shaking, human knees,
Humorously settles down,
Deriding with his infinite, mad eyes
    Our market risk, our saints' unknown.

THE NATIVITY

We are told how the Son of Man was born,
    Known to His Father, Who never
Recognises birth or death; and how the worn
    World's to be His breath forever.

CHRIST TAKES LEAVE OF HIS MOTHEX

He, Who was born of Her that knew not Nature,
Yet with shut fists weeps like Nature's creature;
The black skies resent their shuddering wings,
And what was heavenly weeps, what natural sings.

9

CHRIST'S ENTRY INTO JERUSALEM

Open the gates and welcome in the Lord!
His sweet brow and invisible sword.

Now the palms wither, and the arch
Befriends no more the trulls' and porters' march.

Caesar takes the show seriously—
But Christ is serious with a world to free.

CHRIST EXPELS THE MERCHANTS FROM

THE TEMPLE
The salesmen of ideas fake their list,
Worse than the trulls and their traffickers!
Again and again He strikes them off the list—
Again and again they claim the place as theirs.

WASHING OF THE FEET

With false and annual humility,
Contracting singular love into its type,
The Pharisees extend their feet, which He
In saintly rage will wash, and even wipe!

THE LAST SUPPER

None of us can remember without tears
Nor asking with what faculty we failed:
Was it the purse, or Peter's doubting ears?
        Or the rash brethren jailed?

And when Judas wiped his mouth with bread:
What horror was it raised our loyal arm?
The small room was filled with all the dead;
And Christ broke bread and broke the mortal charm.

Outside the window, the world was still,
Absence of principalities and powers:
        The world His will,
He broke bread and said He would be ours.

Peter and James and John.
Though the fox find shelter and the swollen famished
    dog
And in His dispensation sleep the innocent log,
Yet the Lord finds no breast to lean upon.

Peter and James and John.
Olive branches mime against the moonlight
All natural agitation from sound to sight:
Yet there is not pain enough in Nature for Him to
    reason on.

Peter and James and John.
It is not angels He wants, nor fallen angels even,
    but men
To wear down, if only in Time, that unnatural pain;
Not active Peter, nor neutral James, nor passive John.

CHRIST BEFORE THE MAGISTRATES

By now the Church and State have had their fling,
The generous flesh is pared to the bone:
Christ and Caesar come to the same thing,
    The scorned and scornful soul, their own.

There will be something more when this is over,
The Lion and the Lamb adopt His voice,
    Beloved submit to lover,
Kneel down, and then stand up and rejoice!

VERONICA'S VEIL

They tend His fierce divinity, shy saviours,
From the calvaries of the dispossessed,
Ragged mothers who give milk to their neighbours
While the husband fails, and the child undressed

Scrabbles at the empty plate, some holy women
Will take their last white linen from the drawer
And saying: "God is ours as He is human,"
Wipe the blood from the unbearable scar.

BEFORE PILATE

To flagellate, to crown with thorns, to make
A show of man who would Man create—
Nothing much when Justice is at stake—
The conflict of laws idly becomes Fate.

The scene's complete! the filthy, wine-lit bands
Forgive Barabbas who shed blood,
Pilate, the surgeon, cleans his distant hands,
In sage disgust, praises the Good.

WAY OF THE CROSS

At every stage along that station,
Averted eyes, reluctant heart!
Mob hatred, Pharisees' elation—
His knees watery from the start,

One, Simon, in excess of passion,
Trusted his unreflecting hands;
What is this genius of compassion
That comprehends, nor understands!

AT CALVARY

Axes shone in the sunlight
Where sound and sight from one source came;
Christ was striking at the roots
Whence grew our birthright and its name,

The reason that was perfect gave
The round, simple, pagan sun:
What was humanity to save
The tears of Christ in the machine?

LIFTED ON THE CROSS

There's little certain—but no doubt
Eternity in Time's put out!

There may be lights over the plain,
That's where some acolytes, mad and sane,

Mad for life and sane for death:
Centurion! crown these ribs of wrath!

THE CROSS

Two thieves—why two? to make three criminals?
How dare the centre judge the left and right
Judging: "You shall be with Me in Paradise"
Judging: "You shall be in Hell for life"
If I were one of those two casual thieves
And spied on our degraded bloody Lord:
How could I know how to pronounce the Word,
The Word that doubts, the Word that believes?

THE GOOD THIEF

It is not right for me to talk to You,
To wait on You with ministerial bow,
To pray, or if I lived in higher merit
To love even, or to adore, or care.
Why? the reasons? there are many of them;
        That You are there and are not there.

The huge and foreign universes round me,
The small dishonours in me coat my heart:
Whether the whim of the ignoble beast
Or the Gothic nobility of the choir,
It makes no difference, both high and low,
        Are burned to nothing in Your fire.

My will You will for a fire towards You
Dies without my kindling, or is quenched
In unguided storms from Your high quarters:
My memory in lethargy turns sour
All whence, my understanding less imperious
        Day by day and hour by hour,

Loses whole continents where in my childhood
I was Your Viceroy, and approved the Just
And condemned my natural evil thoughts—

13

Now, what has changed me? Is it the years
You made and gave me, Lord? or am I prone to the evil
    The masters dinned into my ears?

Praise and recrimination sit well on us
Whose quality's defined by life and death;
But nothing, neither life or death adorns us
Like adoration of our Lord, the Christ,
No buildings, no culture of roses, no bridges
    Like the majesty of Christ.

THE BAD THIEF

Lord, we You've made it in our power
To destroy the World You saved us in
And not only our bodies with Your souls,
Your soul created for Your praise forever
But all that has been made against Your image
    Passes, both now and never,

Beasts that eat their young in innocence,
Men that torture knowing what they do—
Innocent things and conscientious things—
We who destroy the flower and the grass,
The thrush whose song's as powerful as the sea
    All this and more has come to pass.

ASCENSION

It happens through the blond window, the trees
With diverse leaves divide the light, light birds;
Aengus, the God of Love, my shoulders brushed
With birds, you could say lark or thrush or thieves

And not be right yet—or ever right—
For it was God's Son foreign to our moor:
When I looked out the window, all was white,
And what's beloved in the heart was sure,

With such a certainty ascended He,
The Son of Man who deigned Himself to be:

14

Then when we lifted out of sleep, there was
Life with its dark, and love above the laws.

TRANSFIGURATION

All is as if that Face transpired with Light
As if dark were light
As if wrong were right
The torsion and the tension of that Night!

The world opens like a door: Come in!
Body is in the way,
Soul is waste and play,
Oh, come, Unworldly, from the World within!

THE TOMB OF MICHAEL COLLINS
to Ignazio Silone

Much I remember of the death of men,
But his I most remember, most of all,
More than the familiar and forgetful
Ghosts who leave our memory too soon—
Oh, what voracious fathers bore him down!

It was all sky and heather, wet and rock,
No one was there but larks and stiff-legged hares
And flowers bloodstained. Then, Oh, our shame
    so massive
Only a God embraced it and the angel
Whose hurt and misty rifle shot him down.

One by one the enemy dies off;
As the sun grows old, the dead increase,
We love the more the further from we're born!
The bullet found him where the bullet ceased,
And Gael and Gall went inconspicuous down.

II

There are the Four Green Fields we loved in boyhood,
There are some reasons it's no loss to die for:

15

Even it's no loss to die for having lived;
It is inside our life the angel happens
Life, the gift that God accepts or not,

Which Michael took with hand, with harsh, grey eyes,
He was loved by women and by men,
He fought a week of Sundays and by night
He asked what happened and he knew what was—
O Lord! how right that them you love die young!

He's what I was when by the chiming river
Two loyal children long ago embraced—
But what I was is one thing, what remember
Another thing, how memory becomes knowledge—
Most I remember him, how man is courage.

And sad, Oh sad, that glen with one thin stream
He met his death in; and a farmer told me
There was but one small bird to shoot: it sang
"Better Beast and know your end, and die
Than Man with murderous angels in his head."

III

I tell these tales—I was twelve years old that time.
Those of the past were heroes in my mind:
Edward the Bruce whose brother Robert made him
Of Ireland, King; Wolfe Tone and Silken Thomas
And Prince Red Hugh O'Donnell most of all.

The newsboys knew and the apple and orange women
Where was his shifty lodging Tuesday night;
No one betrayed him to the foreigner,
No Protestant or Catholic broke and ran
But murmured in their heart: here was a man!

Then came that mortal day he lost and laughed at,
He knew it as he left the armoured car;
The sky held in its rain and kept its breath;
Over the Liffey and the Lee, the gulls,
They told his fortune which he knew, his death.

Walking to Vespers in my Jesuit school,
The sky was come and gone: "O Captain,
    my Captain!"
Walt Whitman was the lesson that afternoon—
How sometimes death magnifies him who dies,
And some, though mortal, have achieved their race.

THE COLOURS OF LOVE
to my wife Caren

Women that are loved are more than loveable,
    Their beauty absolute blows:
But little, like the urgent, carnal soul,
    More than its leaves so mortal in the rose.

O rose! O more than red mortality!
    What can my love have said
That made me her imagine more than be?
    Her mind more than mind, blood more than red?

As the noise of cars and chariots fades,
    And the empire of the stars
Reconquers with its bright and lusty blades
    My room, and heals my scars,

I raise my arms to that mistress planet,
    Venus, whose hunting priests explain
My heart and the rush of legend on it,
    Making me man again!

Those beautiful women shone against the dark
With flowers upon the breast, and birds
Disturbed by foreknowledge, sang some notes.
There were unshed tears, reproach and fret;
I wondered if their women's time was yet.

And the flowers like milk in a dark pantry at night
Offered themselves to the groping hand:
The cliffs fell faster than tears
Reaching that pain where feeling does not matter;
Nor through the house the ghosts' averse patter,

17

Repeating their old theme of the unknown
Birds or women never did translate:
It was as if eternity were breathing
Through the small breathing of the flowers
Shining upon its breast with speechless light.

Remember! do you think I could forget?
The pigeons growl like dogs in sleep remote.
Yet now if you should ask, I could not yet
Forswear that fascination, break that note

Which death in his lush garden exercised,
The habit of repentance feeds the sin,
I know that sloth the solitaries disguised,
I know the door the sweet fogs entered in.

As memory more fitful daylight makes,
Death can increase his holdings in my sleep:
While benched and cheery drunks pull up their stakes
For one more day in search of food and keep.

Abundant stone figures sun themselves
In the precarious granary of the light,
Husbanded by our father, our farmer, selves
Against subversive, supernatural blight.

Voices from the shrubbery nearby:
"Smile with your eyes," one says, "what sweet
      invention!"
What did that Mediterranean nymph reply?
"Smile with your fables and their sweet intention."

Listen in the gold confusion of the wheat,
Inside mortality, to what can move you:
The protests, the protection, the defeat—
"When I am gone," the voice asks, "who will
      love you?"

The crackling lightwaves overhead
Minimise our human year.
O blond haunches! O white bed!
O harmless, ultramundane fear!

Refuge of sinners! Night by night!
Bury your head beneath the sheet:
Still the unworldly angels fight
And casually tear their meat.

It cannot well be said of love and death
That love is better and that death is worse,
Unless we buy death off with loving breath
So he may rent his beauty with our purse.

But is that beauty, is that beauty death?
No, it's the mask by which we're drawn to him,
It is with our consent death finds his breath;
Love is death's beauty and annexes him.

While pestilence feathered down, the hero wasted
Nor would he "cry aloud" or "breathe a prayer"
It being essential to the gall he tasted
That bitterness only bitterness can share.

How could he climb the glen through ruined farms
Nor hear his dead fathers take up arms?
He is a hero, and must make his peace
With all that's left—a few unfrocked police!

I think of seal-barking seas in the West,
It's all between a cry and a caress,
Where the windy islands yield no yeast
And men bake their own bread of bitterness;

Carry the soil of salvation in their arms
Lay it on rock and put down the seed,
It's all in a bed that chills and warms
With too much brood and too little feed.

I saw him move among the iron leaves
Which were to carbonise through his love's breast.
Hers, and the graves of lechers, louts and thieves,
Would sag and musty change be all their rest.

19

When leaves have fallen and there's nothing left
But plainsong from ascetic bony birds,
I say a prayer for all who are bereft
Of love, of leafy summer, of loving words.

I met a kinsman in the market-place,
Singing, and as he sang my courage grew,
It was about betrayal and disgrace,
He said "Love fails but love of love stays true".

Singing in vain and formal in the shade
The noble poverty those houses made.

Divinities of my youth,
Expound to me my truth;

Whether from Judah or Rome
Or my nearer Gaeldom.

The driven horse formalises
His speed for prestige and for prizes,

The girl swinging on the swing
Of the convent, makes me sing

And apples drop like centuries from
The tree of life, so long in bloom;

But divinities of my youth,
You can no longer tell the truth,

It is too much a struggle to
Keep quality confined to you.

When Spring with her lambs and sea-cries rises,
Her fluent fantasy makes a mock of me;
I throw off my absolutist devices
And dissemble in the loose, resplendent sea:

Yet think on how San Juan, bitter and bare,
Wrapt in his drama, sent his cry above,
And though, through layer on suffocating layer
Nothing came back, he loved; and so I love.

At the Bar du Départ drink farewell
And say no word you'll be remembered by;
Nor Prince nor President can ever tell
Where love ends or when it does or why.

Down the boulevard the lights come forth
Like my rainflowers trembling all through Spring,
Blue and Yellow in the Celtic North . . .
The stone's ripple weakens, ring by ring.

Better no love than love, which, through loving
Leads to no love. The ripples come to rest . . .
Ah me! how all that young year I was moving
To take her dissolution to my breast!

THE HEAVENLY FOREIGNER

The face of one I loved and one befriended

Ghosts fill the dark air
Attempting to recover lost ground
Like our repentances, divine and human,
The Street-lamps pad away with failing whisper
And stars more or less when you look at them, like ghosts
Pains and penalties of all men repeat, repeat
Like the people in the Gospels
And the ghosts of the dead and living weave through them all
Women vanish when their hands are tired
In the night-bar, black and red;
And the gold of the hair of a girl entering brings me back
The noon, all that placid light- veiling lucid shadow . . .
While I weep somewhere in the distance . . .
Ah how, in a blue-wind street above the sea,
Against the sun, talking and listening, she bore an idol
    honey-coloured, abstracted out of cell by money-yellow
    cell and fish-scale eyes;
All tales of childhood led me to an idol:
Or how, the time she startled, at evening,
Out of the bloody underbush
After the badger's death, being after being
Being after being of light, on wings and with one sound,

(rising which sounded Beauty! Beauty! and falling
Faith! Faith!.) and out there between the sea and
the sun, some love-goddess clung like a lark to
the clear air.
It was being in the making of heaven, intoned in the
terrestrial
Rehearsal of the faithful, being with her.
The red-cheeked faithful, busy with hope. Yet
If in such heaven my difference should compose,
And in such temporal harmony of health and harm
Flood of perfection flood back over me, there,
There in that bubble I'd exaggerate
A wet meniscus of discontent
And all my activity lie
Chaffing between diameter and arc.
Time virtual is what keeps me in Time:
Leave me in abeyance.

Cathedral close, lawn green as a fairy godmother kirtle
Along the foot of the buttresses,
Some fewscore unregulated graves.
She walked slowly, reading and speaking recitals
For they spoke out of stone
As undeniable as a clerk walks out of a red suburban street
to his daily rubrics;
They filed with the evidence
Their good deeds, their pious influence . . .
Who moves there? who does not move?
What insensate leg fails to twitch away from the mad,
unphonetic worms?
Catherine, it says, Catherine
Whom now an afflicted husband mourns.
It was before and after the needling of the old hair-splitter
from the dark,
The thing behind your elbow;
And there were two, always in soft sunlight drawn close
Together, so by the sensuality of all the particles
and particulars of nature
In such an embrace of space that the thrust of sunlight
in the failing wind and the lapse back of the little
winds upon the summotes took place at the same
time and the same place.
The spires, firm on their monster feet rose light and thin

and trembling in the tracery of bird-motion
and bell-echo;
A woodshaving sailed on the calm, vernal water
Now, fixing our secret in my eyes, that's what is there,
That's what is there, she said, all this is more
Beautiful than Chartres.
Again, again protesting
Like those who will not surrender a small liberty
Which they cannot cultivate in any case.
Rebellion is imperfection like all matter
Mirror without reflection, I am helpless
As if I were watching a wooden beam pushing up through
    the soil
As if I were the soft-voiced people forever against the
    people with hard voices.

Whereas, O my term, my unavoidable turnstile
In the cathedral porch impalpable,
Term itself, apse itself, had you but come,
Our absolute lord had not been me, not I nor you.
But an instant preconising eternity
Borne between our open eyes
With no preceptible bank of land between
Nor oblique eyesight deciding other objects were there.

Come back! come back! your absence cause for tears.
Come back! no cause for fear.
Youth's faithfulness with which I failed you most
Is changed now to a gentler way of seeing
So well I can be faithful to a ghost.

Mostly there's one that loves and one lets love:
But our two appetites devoured their food;
Yet join me in this company I keep:
Not life but below it or above
Where bodiless blind eyes seem to weep.

Day, hot and grey, low over the plains of storm-sogged wheat.
Sky parturient with rain.
And all my laughter ripped out of me and thrown aside
Like the sickened squads of wheat; all my gifts to her!

Rodents in the corn like the black gas in the heart of the sun

The chase and the loving under the damp ditch
Her blond laughter now indecent, her sexual
Ascetic face with the bones loosened

The first rejection is the first injustice
And inadmissable then the crisp, indifferent blow
By turn; the flesh gone fire and the bones gone wood
The brain stutters and stops.

I am the eldest son and my right was questioned
My patrimony drained
I blackened with hatred
As the trees ached intolerably through all their branches
While the laughter was muffed
And the mud crackled round the mounting pulse.

It goes on all night, the sorceresses whispering
Wind in the wood, and when you listen
Vanishing like a whistle downriver. Then, Oh, cling
Close to the world and her; she crowns
This moment with the diadem of her Time, and waves
The floral barge into a frame of trees;
Her eyes darken with the music,
Darkness lies against her mouth,
There is a sharp wind between laugh and cry.

Last night on the gilded Bourbon bridge
The doom of Adam brought me down to earth
While the houses with their worn freight
Filed down the flowing, muttering river.
I was not guilty, had I but known it.
But now and then the royal pall of peace
Falls without prayer, without need,
Love's earnest gift being frivolously given;
And as the lucid, pagan music
Blows with brown leaves over the asphalt,
Guilt slips off like a wet coat in the hall.

... And past her ivory head
Stream the pebble notes like a run of deer;
A shy god moves across the terrace,
A being born among the flowers of her mind
Beautiful, loving and beloved.

24

In all these one-room flats, while the street-lamps
    unseasonably awake all night long
Mutter their proverbs—and it's not worth it, it makes
    no difference—
How many white-collar clerks sit alone over a thin drink
Singing ballads out of anthologies,
Reading, in a spurt and laze of unconvinced enthusiasm,
The Essays of Elia, the novels of Maxim Gorky! and
    brush their teeth,
Take two asprins and fall between the soiled sheets,
Thinking of the good brother and sister who have stayed
    at home
In the country, where the trucks are loading now
With greens and tuberose and cackle
And fall asleep and eagerly enter the dream
Of the church of childhood
Of the campaigns of childhood in the family
For love and rewards of valour.

My beloved is sad, my beloved lays her cheek upon my hand,
    my beloved is sad, sad, my beloved is fearful for us
      "I fear for us" she says
"Where are the masses of little liquid bells, they used
    to ride through the snowy curtains:
Where are the reindeer that agitate their tresses of bells"
And I say:
"Look out through the window again
It is mealtime at midday
Do you see the minimum buses coming to berth at
    the pavements
Do you see the experts trip gaily down the steps on
    helpless marionette legs across the square?
Doesn't this amuse you just as much?"
And she says:
"It does; it does; it is beyond compare; what do I care?"

The snow climbed into the white sky
Plains of desolation above the eyes
Each inch and acre more and more dead
A white inexorable hound.
Lord of the cold! Lord! Friend! stop-heart Lord, stop-brain
    Lord! to be assumed into the love of a celestrial Lord
What pleasure, the stripping of rumination,

A shard which though it protects, yet
Rots our matter.

What head thrown back!
That I need see the equal human,
The natural surroundings of my earthly rank, breast
    to the sun, legs refeshed with wind
Giving in, stepping down.
But I cannot, for the heavens do open, as far, so far as
    I can see.
I will kneel
My genuflection shall sign my faith like a hidalgo before
    his emblem,
Making her the absolute woman of a moment.

Give me your hand, let me help you over the fence.
If you touch a wire, snow will shirr up and fall round you
    like hundreds of eyelids closing, saying with
    understanding, I know, I know:
If you know, why will you try to avoid me in your
    flimsy heart
No more secure than net of snow?
Well you've gussed it, round tree, stone and wave . . . .
That your brighteyed challange draws me on only,
    your diamond moods.
Now our feet must reach the ground, our cadence into
    one another ineluctable,
What peaceful arms were we stilled, burning in snow!

When women leave, with the sky darkening like violets
    in their eyes, they step clear and look sideways, the
    fingers trailing over the horse's flank;
Morning calls, evening falls quiet.
Yesterday it was the flesh; fruit and flower and in the eyes
    concentrated all that is straight, all that dares not ignore
    the oblique floor of death; yesterday she being there,
    when it was love;
Then it was nothing more and nothing less; but now, she
    being gone, the more thickens and the less thins,
The more of affairs, the fattening jowl; the bow to senior
    and the blow to junior; the casual unwilled depths of
    the poem and harvest not miraculous after the sower.
    The father and mother, none of these

None of these: why none? what's all rejection
But courage sputtring out in ageing blood?

Nothing less it was then; and now, O warning from
     nowhere
Nothing less it is now than you, there's no, no
Backing away from that invisible rider's rein;
None of these gifts or gains or losses turned over and over
Till they shine like gains, but that divine
Dissidence in river and wheat
Wet stone, horse unharnessed
Corrupts the smile of the harvest:
And it's no use turning aside, no use
Staring through gray windows
At the bent rain
Slanting on grey seas.

As the sun stands there at one word
And the awakened eye owns all creation
So was she
So was she lord created, prisoner made,
Strong as a fortress, shining as an early fortress.

But the future like a flock of insurance clerks
Came cawing throughout my branches
How long these green, ungrown and candid leaves –
How I might make my soul
In a freedom that might destroy it?
How my busy, alien eye and lip
Might graft and gratify her eye and lip
How the irritant perfect would flush out
Leaving our imperfections gape?

These questions pondering, I pulled up short
Like, against the breakwater of humanity, the shameful,
     unrealised, sad-eyed, animals
While the fiery circle cataracting outerworld
Showed in cold, peaceful stars to our little world
In its circular band of frisky, divine air
In which we build basilicas
And sicken at the sight of two-headed calves.

In the memory, years interweave; they do not follow one
     another

Like jealous ambassadors in the Mayor's procession
All years flow from a hundred streets
Intemperately towards the mansion
Last year no less than this
For her mercurial year threads through them all since;
Since her year like children:
As down an esplanade a Sunday afternoon
The couple descend, assembling their anonymity
And in their mind's maze is hidden a maze with children
    playing
Their flat, white voices rising like kites up above
Their peripatetic manoeuvres and aerial constructions
From which we are as far
As from ants in their odyssies, hidden from view.
Ants are not to be believed
A straight line, self-righteous, impossible,
But children like the thought of flowers come free
In the mind's upper room of luck
With furies and prophecies outside ours
A senselessness of marionette and myth;
But they scream, smile and flit.

Like, by a deathbed,
The multiple silence of the witness
While the testator is scoring his point over death;
Like the thought of birth and death rounding off a
    beautiful form
Like heart to heart
She who was like love-children born.

The years weave through me and young men spend
    their time,
Evenings of unhappiness, a great weak iris . . .
    Time does not stretch ahead of me
As if I might unroll my scroll on it
But it is volumed round me, thick with echoes, things
I cannot see throughout.
Such things so and so many years ago:
The already is my present unresolved.
Separate and self-absorbed, the friends growing older,
Return from the central mystery in the maze
To the primitive blaze of the virgin at the door;
And the mistresses of dead politicos, by the shining lakeside,

Fade, like the hatred in which their Chief went down;
So life both flares and fades in me without her —
Or no, not quite; when I think of a white
Dress along the battlements above the star-broken sea,
Or white lips in the dark stair-well, life without her
Is reading the table of contents without the book.

This I knew
When the children were ghosts by the lakeside,
The woman a ghost doll in the palm of my hand:
She was not the perfectability
Of wrinkled or lariat-chanced virtue:
No need to think of her but as separate;

No need to make of her
Any invisible, ideal vampire
Sucking my cells that water anyway.
Night is wide and without definition
One or two recognitions heard spoken
Fallen valleys of silence between,
Evening falls past the window and eyes glow.
Young men will not name the beloved object for fear of
    degrading it.
Mental prayer is the highest ... And just that point
Which is only and nothing else yourself
Is that point, is that which I love
With no words for it.

Since the time in childhood
When dishes gleamed on the dresser,
And the tall, blue benignant
And black, malignant ghosts
Meant what they said,
Blue for heaven's haven
Black for the fear of hell;

A boy on a blond crate
Outside the sunlit stables
Under sheets of silence
Spoke low to the large-eyed racehorse;
Before that Eldest Son
Had heard of the Princess,
Before the Flood

Had washed the world's kidneys,
When eyes grew brighter and brighter
And tears of generosity
Were in suprise created
Out of the musing flesh:

There spoke something else —
But the sense escaped me —
And if we were in sin,
Sad or joyful sin,
Singing or sighing
Round the corner of the eye —
Round the invisible back:
Since the time in the back field
The vast copper beech,
With the pronged sensibility
Of his thousand leaves,
Received and weaved and changed
Logical shafts of light
And modulating rain
And through his roots, rain rising
Like a diver back;
Or from the beach at evening
The sea like a musing spider:
Both thousand leaves and sea
Sang something else,
Shone something else;
Since men can have said
On their bed of death —
"I have made women happy!"
Or, "that was in my good days,
I bred a handsome filly!"
Or, "I lowered the price of bread,
A new-elected Minister!"
Or, "with my love I loved
Those who gave their lives!"

Something there was other
Always at my elbow,
I sang, hunted and hated one;
He sings and hunts and hates me;
Say heaven or hell
Well or ill

I cannot make it different,
Anything, or even other.

O day of labour!
O day of labour and spit in which I was cast down and
     raised up!
When the foreign power intervened and made all the
     difference
Between the bog and the road,
Making the present, making life
Where the bull is silent in his shadow
And the farmhouse in its handmaid ring of trees;

There is the light small in the dark;
There is the heart filled with oil which will burn,
Which will be quenched.
The world glows with mortal divinity;
The red turns gray,
The ash creeps up on the flame
O heavenly foreigner! your price is high.

There is nothing now that will buy him off;
The singers of life who are the memory of life
Are silenced by the scream of plant, tree, sea;
The beautiful severed head floats downriver;
The land recedes
With all its needy industry of wheat and vine;
With her weaving spells out of the spell of her speech.
Weaving charm out of the charm of her body;
The day recedes with all my adorations.

How she stood, hypothetical-eyed and metaphor-breasted
Weaving my vision out of my sight
Out of my sight, out of my very sight,
Out of her sight
Till the sight it sees with is blind with light
Other than hers, other than mine
Till it unravels
And there's only a light smoke in my hands

And this is where, O bed of beds!
Tiger, rough of skin and smooth of eye!
She is my loss and my lost one

And I will possess and dare, cannot possess
This other one, this similar, this one.

Like all rivers with their diverse chimes hurrying towards
    the sea
So all my be and are towards you.
There is none but you I think of.
I know there is one thing, which is you, it is the unique
Which also in part is she,
You, not seen by her,
You, not to be reduced by my eyes' famine of her.
She and I the Rest I absorbed in you
And well you know it; a night like this tramps off, its
    footsteps made ridiculous by comparison with the vast
    talking page it rolls its black, schoolman ruler over,
    five-thousand year China and then Russia and then
    Central European time, round and round the world
    accompanied by the lights we make and the dreams
    closed in our humble sleep.
Well you know it, the end I mean.
It is that by which you know the anguished communication
    between us.
Being of my being, say of my say
We are pulled up short by death,
Our hands signal by the same high-voltage wire;
Like the mob which stampedes across a racecourse and is
    pulled up at the palisade, its members turning,
    regarding each other, suprised into violent
    introduction;
And know themselves—with eye and skull, with skeleton.
As I know you, there, behind my back. As I know as far as
    I can think and have thought you
There is none so much as you, none you, I think of.

II

LOUGH DERG AND OTHER POEMS
(1946)

LOUGH DERG

The poor in spirit on their rosary rounds,
The jobbers with their whiskey-angered eyes,
The pink bank clerks, the tip-hat papal counts,
And drab, kind women their tonsured mockery tries,
Glad invalids on penitential feet
Walk the Lord's majesty like their village street.

With mullioned Europe shattered, this Northwest,
Rude-sainted isle would pray it whole again:
(Peasant Apollo! Troy is worn to rest.)
Europe that humanized the sacred bane
Of God's chance who yet laughed in his mind
And balanced thief and saint: were they this kind?

Low rocks, a few weasels, lake
Like a field of burnt gorse; the rooks caw;
Ours, passive, for man's gradual wisdom take
Firefly instinct dreamed out into law;
The prophets' jeweled kingdom down at heel
Fires no Augustine here. Inert, they kneel;

All is simple and symbol in their world,
The incomprehended rendered fabulous.
Sin teases life whose natural fruits withheld
Sour the deprived nor bloom for timely loss:
Clan Jansen! less what magnanimity leavens
Man's wept-out, fitful, magniloquent heavens

Where prayer was praise, O Lord! the Temple trumpets
Cascaded down Thy sunny pavilions of air,
The scroll-tongued priests, the galvanic strumpets,
All clash and stridency gloomed upon Thy stair;
The pharisees, the exalted boy their power
Sensually psalmed in Thee, their coming hour!

And to the sun, earth turned her flower of sex,
Acanthus in the architects' limpid angles;
Close priests allegorized the Orphic egg's
Brood, and from the Academy, tolerant wranglers
Could hear the contemplatives of the Tragic Choir
Drain off man's sanguine, pastoral death-desire.

It was said stone dreams and animal sleeps and man
Is awake; but sleep with its drama on us bred
Animal articulate, only somnambulist can
Conscience like Cawdor give the blood its head
For the dim moors to reign through druids again.
O first geometer! tangent-feelered brain

Clearing by inches the encircled eyes,
Bolder than the peasant tiger whose autumn beauty
Sags in the expletive kill, or the sacrifice
Of dearth puffed positive in the stance of duty
With which these pilgrims would propitiate
Their fears; no leafy, medieval state

Of paschal cathedrals backed on earthy hooves
Against the craftsmen's primary-coloured skies
Whose gold was Gabriel on the patient roofs,
The parabled windows taught the dead to rise,
And Christ the Centaur in two natures whole,
With fable and proverb joinered body and soul.

Water withers from the oars. The pilgrims blacken
Out of the boats to masticate their sin
Where Dante smelled among the stones and bracken
The door to Hell (O harder Hell where pain
Is earthed, a casuist sanctuary of guilt!).
Spirit bureaucracy on a bet built

Part by this race when monks in convents of coracles
For the Merovingian centuries left their land,
Belled, fragrant; and honest in their oracles
Bespoke the grace to give without demand,
Martyrs Heaven winged nor tempted with reward.
And not ours, doughed in dogma, who never have dared

Will with surrogate palm distribute hope:
No better nor worse than I who, in my books,
Have angered at the stake with Bruno and, by the rope
Watt Tyler swung from, leagued with shifty looks
To fuse the next rebellion with the desperate
Serfs in the sane need to eat and get;

Have praised, on its thunderous canvas, the Florentine smile

As man took to wearing his death, his own
Sapped crisis through cathedral branches (while
Flesh groped loud round dissenting skeleton)
In soul, reborn as body's appetite:
Now languisht back in body's amber light,

Now is consumed. O earthly paradise!
Hell is to know our natural empire used
Wrong, by mind's moulting, brute divinities.
The vanishing tiger's saved, his blood transfused.
Kent is for Jutes again and Glasgow town
Burns high enough to screen the stars and moon.

Well may they cry who have been robbed, their wasting
Shares in justice legally lowered until
Man his own actor, matrix, mould and casting,
Or man, God's image, sees, his idol spill.
Say it was pride that did it, or virtue's brief:
To them that suffer it is no relief.

All indiscriminate, man, stone, animal
Are woken up in nightmare. What John the Blind
From Patmos saw works and we speak it. Not all
The men of God nor the priests of mankind
Can mend or explain the good and broke, not one
Generous with love prove communion.

Behind the eyes the winged ascension flags,
For want of spirit by the market blurbed,
And if hands touch, such fraternity sags
Frightened this side the dikes of death disturbed
Like Aran Islands' bibulous, unclean seas:
Pieta: but the limbs ache; it is not peace.

Then to see less, look little, let hearts' hunger
Feed on water and berries. The pilgrims sing:
Life will fare well from elder to younger,
Though courage fail in a world-end, rosary ring.
Courage kills its practitioners and we live,
Nothing forgotten, nothing to forgive.

We pray to ourself. The metal moon, unspent
Virgin eternity sleeping in the mind,

37

Excites the form of prayer without content;
Whitehorn lightens, delicate and blind,
The negro mountain, and so, knelt on her sod,
This woman beside me murmuring *My God! My God!*

ENCOUNTER

"Our saints are poets, Milton and Blake,
Who would rib men with pride against the spite
Of God," the Englishman said, and in the silence
Hatred sparkled along our bones. He said:
"Celt, your saints adorn the poor with roses
And praise God for standing still."

Between the two of us, François from Touraine,
Where women and the wheat ripen and fall due
Suavely at evening, smiled, teasing the breadcrumbs.
He whispered: "Patience; listen to the world's
Growth, rustling in fire and childlike water!"

And I: "Milton and Marvell, like the toady, Horace,
Praised the men of power for the good
They happened on, with bible and sword; the wretched
Hold out their begging-bowls at the wooden gates,
Too poor to weep, too poor to weep with tears."

Boxflower scent. Fumes of burgundy.
Nagging children at the tables
A dream's remove from their fathers smoking
Along the boulevard laid with yellow evening.

FROM GOVERNMENT BUILDINGS

Evening lapses. No pity or pain, the badgered
Great get home, and the little, tomorrow's anchorage,
All smiling, sour the milk of charity,
Like the pyrrhonist poets, Love's saboteurs.

The clerks fan out and the lamps; and I look inwards:
What turns amuse you now? with whom, not me! do
You cower in Time, whose palsied pulse is nimbler
A hair's breadth when want and have are equal?

38

My room sighs empty with malignant waiting;
The November wind slows down outside, wheeling
Twig and awning on the brick balcony,
A wind with hackles up. In Rome at evening

Swallows traced eggshapes on the vellum sky,
The wind was warm with blue rain in Dublin;
When the culture-heroes explored the nether world
It was voiceless beasts on the move made Death terrible.

Friendship I will not, barring you; to have witness does:
Doll birds, dogs with their social nose, by day
Are touchstone. But at night my totem silence
With face of wood refuses to testify.

The famous exile's dead, from many on many
Deportations, from Spain to Prague to Nice,
Kaleidosdopic police, his Danse Macabre;
One of the best the worst had never feared.

You, you I cherish with my learned heart
As in the bombed cathedral town, doubly
A tourist trophy now, the dean shouted: "At last!
At least and at last we have stored the windows away,

The fabulation of my Lord's glory, by
Seven and by seven and by seven multiplied!"
So is my care though none your mystic I,
Nor you like the painted saints but breath and more.

And do not pace the room haunting the furniture
But be my insular love; and I would have you
Fingering the ring with its silver bat, the foreign
And credible Chinese symbol of happiness.

THE STATUE AND THE PERTURBED BURGHERS

Emptied and pearly skulls
Lie humbly among the roots of the grass
The inhabitants know it only too well
Walking delicately
Under the trees.

They have stayed this fluttering boy in tight marble
For a fresh similitude
Of their rare immersion in stillness,
Planted foaming trees
For coolness.

People of worth and wealth
Glancing with care at their modes of life,
Walls, cradles, windows, amber orchards.

My watch ticks as loud as a sledgehammer in an empty street.
Muffle the panting hours, my fountain, disdain them,
Boy with the beaked chin.

The tendrils of fountain water thread that silk music
From the hollow of scented shutters
Crimson and blind
Crimson and blind
As though it were my sister
Fireflies on the rosewood
Spinet playing
With barely escaping voice
With arched fastidious wrists to be so gentle.

MEMO FROM A MILLIONAIRE

What jugs, what knives, what cups for drinking in!
My keys! my watch! my silk-protected skin!
Ginger and orange glowing, mouse-foot peas,
My princely delft! my girls with deft, silk knees,
A wineglass feted on the roulette cardboard,
Thumbcurl frescoes veer, veer to starboard
While my steward, with chuckle apples, brings
My guests, whose hunger's punctual as kings,
Beautiful and casual like those masks the sun
Breaks off from burning clouds at his decline.

Take you my food and games, swear at my crew:
I am more than you by what I give to you;
If panic whirled me to unload my shares:
How would these guests convert all bulls to bears,
From their dark brokeries nag at me and nibble

Till my proud plethora crumbled to a dribble!
But better in the meantime rich and rooked
Than poor and pawned and crumb-thrifty and crocked,
Even if my only friends, like my desires,
Are doll outside but, inside, space and wires—
Joseph, that sandy baron, made his pile
In heretic Egypt, God indulged his guile:
Having it both ways, Ghibelline and Guelph?
The money's hard, I would not blame myself.

Time only blame me, Time with outlaw right,
Ambush me in my shadow-slip mind's night;
Mirror my double, merciless: a sinister
Cynical bishop in his empty minster!
"What of that you," Time asks, "wherein you dreamt
Instruments for my meaning and measurement?
These irritating, unseen wings that force
My massive moves, you failed to chart their course."
Ah, Time, unjust! that spawn stars, keys and knives
For your imperious increase, with lives
With seaports and with ships like these, what turning
I took, what time, was of your make and earning.

I have spicked and spanned my life until it shone
Like my crisp steamer with its sunny brain.
Sun, be my shield! disturb not my agreement;
Let the rays fly as far as they are meant
Lest, in the tragic sense, a sweet breast dip
And warn young lovers life springs from a slip:
No door, no door tear out the wall with it,
My house of tricks, last out your siege in habit;
Pretend, my spectrumed ear, to tones, for show,
You cannot really catch, thread to the radio
The escaped canary in the garden tree
Practising with chill chirps a headlong spree
And the dragonfly that hums an unheard noise, as
He procreates in pretty circular poises.

Who sees me, with the dust of my possessions,
Unmoistened mortar, mending Time's abrasions?
Who knows me, lunging at a drunken sock
Jackknifed to daylight by my cock-shriek clock
From my confessional of night, whose phantoms

41

Act out my stunted sainthood, twit my tantrums?
Outfoxed, forsworn, belittled and outbannered!—
If from that good despair I rise, well-mannered
To taunt my dainty guests; with tailored pride
Review my keys, my watch, my ship-flecked tide.

ROYAL CANAL

She will stand in the window any moment now
The world plunged in the evening light
A costly silence between enemies.

The gruff mongrels in aimless exercise
With boys shouting; and then a silence.
All shouting waves around
Silence like a blind egg
Terror fills her old eyes as in girlhood

She turns from the window; her fingers
Feather the keyboard
A brush of melodies
A perspicuous storm of chords
She finishes nothing.

The druid elms, closed in their lost language,
Their shoulders heavy
With a menace not their natural own
Rest in panic on the still canal.

MIXED DRINKS

The whiskey's prurience through the inner pipes.
This is the change and leaving of thy name.

In the fungus of drunken breathing
Mist feels at the mirrors
Like doubt turning to anger
In the judge's face.

Blond beer cylinders weave

42

The waitresses' trays ripple over our heads.
I am alone but the others are with me
Tasting the same food, drink and sleep
After the day of ambush
When anguish made the soul efficient
With bell, book and candle,
When the lie startled like stoats into hiding
In the eyes of butcher, baker and banker,
When death put up a showy magazine front
For officer and ranker.

It is a kind of dream-desecration
Of the most beautiful forms man has imagined:
Yet you feel less defiled than when you see
The uncompetitive horror in the eyes
Of a dying man
A little before death.

A shabby-nosed old drunk
Limns with one loyal, black-gloved hand
The motions of a baton, orchestrating
Out of the oxen heart
The world, the flesh and the devil,
The dare of the trumpets, ivied erosion of theme,
Violin-shell children.

JANSENIST JOURNEY

"Then, We'll go through with the journey," said
My brother and myself, "and bring
With us our black-faced scapegoat, Guilt."

We bested the last lingering hill
Of life; and got donkeys to ride
For it would be long going through the wood.

I was to loose our goat of guilt
At a shameful bypath on the way;
But the brightness turned him innocent:

The donkey's patience through the thorns,
The gay old nurses, the green inns:
He bucked the wild flowers with flashing horns:

43

These freshets garlic to his taste.
But I put no trust in him, no trust.
At last we reached the Gospel gates,

Aching and dirty. Robes lay there.
Mother and sisters like light through glass,
With stopped lightning stood in the arch.

They washed our heads, hands and feet,
In the same low voice they laughed and sobbed,
The mother gave us a diamond each,

Casketed, shut with a miser's clasp,
I said to my brother: "Life, the diamond,
Is locked inside hard and fast."

"Yes?" he said, putting his down
Indifferently. I opened mine:
It was a gold ball. It was sundown,

We entered cloisters with a priest,
Sat on the stone wall, listening
To his plans for our retreat,

Black-face forgotten, the diamond too,
And the mother and sisters. No rapture;
The plain virtue of the chosen few.

CASA BUONAROTI

He struggled all life with pigment, rock, chisel and sun
To put God in matter, magnify himself;
Worked against Time, rhetorical skull on the shelf,
To muscle in stone ideas by Time undone:
And skull's grin, that long bogey, would outrun
His work yielded to Time: why God made Hell:
The inch to retreat to from the daring ell
Of giving his image the risk of being none.

Not devils but the meek minimise the great
Who bind their eyes as likely as not

So not is like what they would like it were.
Samson they enhance us whom our flaws deflate:
Yet God, from the refuge of his comic thought,
Moves the momentary tourist with his fear.

WEST PIER

The master says, Good Dog! and the mailboat
Dips for the start.
The moon's mad, sharp face extracts
From the fields an inadvertent animal wail.

Those two with head to head against the gangway,
Two as close as joined palms, if pulled apart,
Their lifeline will be stopped short and everything
Look different as at night.

Aboriginal anger and Christian terror
Wound happiness. The stevedore
Knifes his way through the port when hurt; the steward
Dims apprehension with the daily rosary,
Life and death all needled on the frail
Manipulations between boat and sea,
The balance tipped over by the slightest finger.

The land trembles like water in the green light.
Damp couples dawdle on the pier,
Their snug paradise to be a giving
And a taking away.
The wicked and the pious, driving, driven
Excuse a withered life by a useful one.

The sea's gamesome voice is seen
A quarter mile out where the promontories
Excoriate its dark glass skin.
I love and lose her with an ever love.

Sleep or death, those canyons come upon
Beneath the moon's debauched, athenian smile,

Will terrify with monstrous theatre
Our anger and our terror.

That screen is mist,
That screen on which you do your lives bedizen,
Two on the gangway, steward and stevedore.

EST PRODEST

Tablelands of ice
Bastions of blocks of light
Are his identity
Or light as flutenotes
At a flick he is round me flowing
Denying, promising,
Boulders of ice, gentian,
Daring, dominant
As a tower drags up the eyes.
Whose eyes will not flare
Jerked out of sloth by sudden
Bugles and flags blaring?
In gentleness, who not answer
The shy, friendly nudging
Of that insistent stallion?
He stamps there, desperate, sweet,
The air aches with our breath.
He is me otherwise.

If One, they all say,
Shows himself in us
Groups of men and women
Mnemonic said of Eden
That stink high in our nostrils
Rich and poor and dead:
Then how darkly he
Is broken among us
In frosty slopes at hazard,
Sunlight on the frangent
Mirrors of the sea.

46

Phrases twisted through other
Reasons reasons disproofs
Identity obscured
Like mirrors shining through other
Reasons reasons disproofs.

Ah, Numberless and Nameless
As mute walls of ivory:
Here question's waste of time.
In extreme pain, painless
The beloved and secure
The clouted sobbing fools
Are stunned in his sleep of thunder
Success or no success
Equal in effortless death:
But days by days are numbered
He must be proved in Time.

Getting away with Love
Dry-lipped love that takes
No action, but battens
On misery, its guest, its prey:
And if the pipes of my nerves
Steam at high tension
Is it then satisfaction?
Alas, that One which loves me
Is my bribe to imperfection
By the muffled brain invented
Is self-love in reflection.

I am blown blown gone foolish
This lung-exhalation
Of now impotent angels
Is useless to usage.

Here, but if here I trample
On the gliding hides of earth
With multitudes trampling:
Then, out of what's superfluous
To its cause in other's agony,
I am sweated into worth
We are all other's work.

He being is freed moving
Seeing and seen in mirrors
We move into being
O miracle moved like children!
Distempered blood soothing;

And deep to my heart whisper
The charged, rippling starfields
Murmur of cities
The maned azure whinneying
Its voices, panic,
Cataracting, bestial,
Breathing beyond my hearing,
Do whirl me off with gold
Serpents and seas and insects
The loosened universe flowing
Loathsome, limpid; there
Shines the eternal horror.

Gaiety and filth of birth!
Bodies grip, eyes' angles
Intersect the multiplicate netting
Of lives distinct and wrangling,
Each knot all others potential,
Friction, spark seminal
Of elders and outlanders.

Mirrors flashing each other:
That's the only proof
Let there be no absence!
The only solution,
Flash between mirrors
Not one, but many, but many!
Reason enough to go on with
And to bind my guides internal
To comb the suspect splendours
Love enough is enough
Presence craving
To speak in my action.

Frightened antinomies!
I have wiped examples from mirrors

I have brought to heel my shadow —
Soul from her rebel heavens
My mirror's face and I
Are like no god and me
My death is my life's plumed gnomon,
Is a bride's embrace cruciform.
Reckless antinomies!
Asymptotes that gasp
Out of your element
You shrink in the sunny mind
Now this fit is on me
And sealed mouths ripping
Tinctured with immediate
Usage which will agree to
No leave of absence
Let out their spate of birds

O fillers in of gaps!
Pure winged linking
To that which reflects me,
The third from the twain distinct not!
Is love of me in action.

His cliffs of ice are melted
Lord, thy wind with pollen!
Green land, be lilied with springs!
Where now my enemies? Gadflies
Dispersed. Favouring wind,
In your muttering silk fans
Winnowing the sundust, bring him!
Lord of delight and absence!
Thy bastions of light are taken
And our eyes like jewelled, subtle
Fish in thee are native
Lord of light shattered
Gathered now in my breast
Lord consubstantial
My pelican brood, my pleasure!

And sky is of his breath
With what tender pressure
He breathes his sky!

Tears from the depths, tears,
Desire glints in the peaks.
Groups of men and women!
Let existence lie female
To our crystal showers, his mirrors
Till, heaven over earth, we shape it
Into his cognation

And he will move breathing
Through us wing-linked
Proleptic of what Eden

Quiet blown in air
Lightened as if we were

HANDY ANDY

OUT of the thighs the bosthoon comes
Blotched and blind and learning fright
To teethe the tigerish, rosy gums,
Fingers to feed the manual sight.

Who died? It was another.
I cried bitter, cried sore
Then got my moor hen in the heather
And slept and cried no more.

BALLAD OF MISTRESS DEATH

"OH, I've had ten men before you,"
Said my readhead Sally,
"Yes, and a hundred men before you,"
Said my new-found darling.
The sea's blue maw glittered
Like a fat barbaric queen's
And her thighs were white and gold
Like wisp-rain in sunshine.
In the long hall with statues
We sat and were not lonely,
Her name all forgotten,

My darkhead, my darling
Said in a gentle voice:
"And you never will be jealous
Though many's the man's head
Has lain upon my pillow,
For you've found out my secret
And many's the man more will."

"Yes, I've found out your secret,"
Walking the dark streets
Through leaf-shaken lamplight.
"I never will be jealous
Nor you numb or nag at me
I'll name you the world's most beauty
Yellowheaded Helen
And no lie be telling;
No woman will disprove it."

She held me like nightfall
Her breath came like knives
While the housing plains sank lower
With their cinder-grates of cities—
Oh, there will need no porters
When all those doors open!

ANK'HOR VAT

The antlered forests
Move down to the sea.
Here the dung-filled jungle pauses

Buddha has covered the walls of the great temple
With the vegetative speed of his imagery

Let us wait, hand in hand

No Western god or saint
Ever smiled with the lissome fury of this god
Who holds in doubt
The wooden stare of Apollo
Our Christian crown of thorns:

There is no mystery in the luminous lines
Of that high, animal face
The smile, sad, humoring and equal
Blesses without obliging
Loves without condescension;
The god, clear as spring-water
Sees through everything, while everything
Flows through him

A fling of flowers here
Whose names I do not know
Downy, scarlet gullets
Green legs yielding and closing

While, at my mental distance from passion,
The prolific divinity of the temple
Is a quiet lettering on vellum.

Let us lie down before him
His look will flow like oil over us.

ON MOUNT MUCKISH

This hill could stage the end-play of a move
Of tribes their lifelong by the sagas haunted,
The peak-led lightning dramatise the roof,
The cairn sum up whole tent-sleep peoples depending
Like us on stones to record the hard-won norm
Through which our race its vagrant passion manned.
Put out of pet now, grooved in cyclic harm,
The close of death is grave, we will not rant.

Faint in the hulabulloo the ghostly tribes
Shake in our fathers' handsome act of death.
Temple, town-hall fall with silent pipes.
All the love-legends of the abandoned earth,
When the intestate loins have spent their race,
Would come to mind with tears and forfeit voice.

MEDITATION AT AVILA

Magnificence, this terse-lit, star-quartz universe,
Woe, waste and magnificence, my soul!

Stand in the window. Fountain waters
Bloom on invisible stems. Soul, my dear friend,
Welcome as always;
Fibrous listener in the darks of mind
Till my confession
Articulate your silence,
Pallas Athene through my beating temples.
Seed, sap and fruit.

You shall see blue arches of emptiness marching into the
        horizon
Over the yellow and black, the intolerant
Excellency of the Castilian highlands
All rock. And the sky
At its looped height
No pick or rope would clamber me up those impalpable
        crags of air!
If I could not talk to you
Fear would oppress me.

The Moroccan traveller says good-night on the marble
        staircase
That rises round the great hall too blank for ghosts.
Flames in the brazier crouch; the hound chitters;
The traveller's housewife
Like a wife too long shut away in a new suburb
Chatters: through her inept words, the epileptic
Sacrifice of black bulls; almond blossom, oranges,
Anxious cultures among the wide, bronze, mountainous
        wastes,
The sigh-spent wavetops of sierras;
Dance, the shellfish eaten, dance, the stertorous heels,
Sensual asseveration of bare thigh:
I stored her joy in my breast against the future.
Good night, the husband stands savouring a well-turned
        jealousy;
The wife

53

Goes to him, sleepy and reluctant.
Contempt falls like a shadow between us.

Look out at the opened sluices of starlight,
Processionless plains with no
Humid corn or trees suckling or spectacular poppies,
Scarce earth but rock
Harsh as the forehead of Jahveh.

Nothing between
Rock and sky.
Santa Teresa
Her choirs of leaf-faced monks
Quavering like plain chant
Chanting to God to down
The Devil, his works and pomps.
The blue, absolute blow
Of linear Castilian night
Cleaves earth and heaven,
God being star-froze heaven
And Devil, fluent earth.
O Santa, Santa Teresa,
Covetous, burning virgin!
Scorning to nourish body's
Farmlands with soul's
Modulating rains,
You lost your eyes' rich holdings
To rubble, snakes and swine
And like the skeptical miser
You lost the usufruct
Of heaven, this floral life,
Hoarding to hasten it over
Death's barren, coughing border.

With fruitful diminution of my light,
Like Eve, accomplisht out of Adam's side,
Soul glides, a glow of flesh, from out its packing.
Much have you left me thus, only to clear me
When chattels and truck of life too much have cumbered,
You, at once the radiance and the kindling
Of dream and deed sown in my travelling.
What is your word for me?

I hear: it is the seed, the sap, the fruit
All flowering in a doomed and sunny moment
From summer to summer; and you bring me
Comfort, my viaticum, journey-food.

Even though the full savour
Is edged with mortality;
And though your saving presence
Is never a promise, comes without warning
Or, being most wanted, fails:
Yet, soul, my long foreboding of the bone
And my green fire fermenting under loam
During the building, eating and sleeping,
When there is no actual advertence,
Thinking, not thinking, thinking of you
In streets of wheaten sunlight

In love's body,
In the look of an old, bleak man
Nearing death
His shut coffer of fear under his arm;
Or when I see in front of the sky a great, sunny angel
Leaning on his elbows over a mountain,
Well may you come,
My self, seed of my suffering, seed
Of my want,
Fallen by the wayside,
Fallen among thorns, seed
Of my faith, my hope and my love!

Do you remember how, one night,
Staring up at the Milky Way,
Simplified like a parish registry recording only life and death,
With an ink-dim memory leafing back the centuries,
I watched the innumerable, witless cortege of the dead
Floating mute and baffled, they had died
All their desires fresh on their hastening lips,
They had gone out the door of life between two calls;
And I thought of the sigh of birdsong, stop and
        woodwind of
Starlings all up and down the green mile in the Ramblas,

While the stars wrinkled like crab apples with humorous,
    blue eyes;

O dead! O dead deprived! whose grief, filling my heart,
Called out for any reason for your rapt,
But called in alien silence, sensitive to
The hale and have of my humanity:
There, as I looked, so all a pity moved me
Groaning, I turned away with clenched fists
And there were you again,
Toothless, bald and smiling.

OLD JACOBIN

The round-backed river
Like a sleek, white cow
Shivers with day arriving
In the light of innocence
The slag is washed away
I make my soul, am peaceful
As though I had never sinned;

Never lied to the people
Lying to themselves
As I flagged them on with promises
Like the lover loving less than the beloved
Looking in her gentle face
Comforting her with lies.
The sun was gone from my father's garden
The white bodies vanished from the stream
And gunmetal twilight steeled my madness;
And I wore the pandemonium of the heroes.
But the antique stuffs I wrapt my virtue in:
Porous they proved to the maleficent winds
When prison walls
Roared in my ears high and black like thunder
The time I signed away the men I loved.
Where were the hero-selves that my imperium
Summoned from the *Odes*, the Roman *Lives*
To walk with me on the lawns in my green time?

Were they our forebears, then, the great dead?
The ghosts of children without bread and milk
Thronged my threshold; their fathers
Wept without tears.
I shouted in the Assembly; the deputies

Blushed in the drama. They knew and I
The Goddess Reason's treasonable trance.
Scarlet fuchsias open their honey
In the linen-pure morning. Here no children
    haunt me—
O chiming, ventral river, if thou were Lethe!
Men of pleasure say I have wronged them
Who wronged themselves; hatred in their eyes
Like poor, shining straw.

The new President will fatten the poor:
But my factions in the misty pubs
Will strike the benches in shame
For the right denial, the personal curse foregone.

Still to quiet the children's crying, how I would give
My one blood and heart! But that was done, Christ!
Nor did that Tree bear like a round apple
The all good here; nevertheless
As the water bears the light equably
And as I will have no shame before my father
I bear my life
Without regret or praise.

Bitter watercress
Long water widening to where
There is but water and light and air.

ANTEROOM: GENEVA

The General Secretary's feet whispered over the red carpet
And stopped, a demure pair, beside the demure
Cadet, poor but correct,

Devoted menial of well-mannered Power.
"A word with you." "Yes, your Excellency."
Excellency smiled. "Your silk shirt is nice, Scriptor.
But listen. Better not let these private letters
Reach the President. He gets worried, you know,
About the personal misfortunes of the people;
And really, the Minister is due to arrive.
It is surely most unseemly
To keep the State in the waiting-room
For God knows what beggars,
For totally unnecessary people."

Their mutual shirtfronts gleamed in a white smile
The electorate at breakfast approved of the war for peace
And the private detective idly deflowered a rose.

ARGUMENT WITH JUSTICE

Virtue all men stand under, what wonder, blinded on thy
    column transcendental, thou art
Sterile, since not bedded with man thy secular wooer who
    could waken thy
Dreams to bloom; and why blinded?
Darest not take, not take to thy sight these anarchic, thy
Realms of thy reign abandoned?

Anchorite of the aether, thy influence in the brain quivers
    but tenuous . . . with what desperate antennae,
    dearest! and thy
Lamps in our breasts fret out; no less does thy bruised
    forehead anger us like the
Great limed birds, Isaiah and Chartres in the
Pensioner hold of thy sisters, cold heraldic
Mercy and Charity sour-dugged.

Widowed of our seed which would leaven and make serial
    thee, marmoreal in the hangings of heaven,
    welcoming
Nature's moan as an ever imminent epithalamium, know
    that, hooded, thy
Dream of will's no will flowering in

Action, blowzed menstruate, wasting till some fancied
Excellence fit thy arrival.

Rigid, breathless to scare not thy death-heeled steps,
      O novice, we should wait thee, as pure and
      dawnlit, thy
Guardians, the elder cliffs of the first country to chant and
      entemple thee,
Born beside an unstrung blue
Sea and trembling its transparence in thy mien, O equable!
O crags and crushed-foam beauty!

Beautiful named because from time abstract and therefore
      sacrosanct? Ah, what good! if the
Cunning have bandaged thee thus with eternity, turned thee
      lodestar blandishing them and the
Innocent in the ignorant ruin of
Kingdoms and fevered republics babbling dry-lipped
Beneath thy blind silence?

Blown, see, against thy portals, centuries of mortals mouth
      blasphemy righteous: "What reward for
Fasting, and why, the future clasped, must the present ring
      of diverse winds puff out in
Vanity? She will not come down
Lest our contentment then should prove her jealous
Heaven untrue." Virtue

Virtue of all men, fear not that we thy temple crumble,
      flesh crumbles, but
Not till the mind's raped out. Fear rather thy name be
      forgotten from father to
Son, or by thy saints. Come down, let there be
Justice though the heavens fall, be virtue of our
Temporary measure.

PAYS CONQUIS

The invader came again and conquered
With the old by-product crimes
But three years later the harvest flaunted,

59

The young kept faith with Time.
The invader built bridges, roads
Feeding the pastures to the ports;
Endowed schools where experts learned
To drain the steam rebellion churned.
The mayor, the general forgot
Jean and Jacques unjustly shot.

And when the careless earth brought forth
Well-fed children, wheat and coal
More than the laws provided for:
The shadowy experts muffed their role;
Jacques in his widow's bed was hate,
The rifles hid by Jean were bared
To win back pride in free estate;
And refuse papers flew in the square
Outside the scared Proconsulate.

BOY BATHING

On the edge of the springboard
A boy poses, columned light
Poised.
Seagulls' crying wrinkles
The brown parchment cliffs.
His body shines: a knife!
Spread wings, he opens
Plunges
Through the gold glass of sunshine
Smashes
In crumbs of glass the silence.

BACCHANAL

Forerunners, with knees flashing like scissors, raced by
    the hostile telegraph wires,
Start for the ships with the news, Cut Through, all is against
    them despair inspires:
The poor made limp by want of cackling, brainstopped
    youth, a seaweed crowd . . .

How the road that smokes through the mountains, whose
    panther-bounding shadows applaud, is loud
With the confident feet of pursuing criers! their eyes
    diamond with thousands of years
Of domination ands lands held of fictitious papers by right of
    fears,
Easy on which to maintain the sneering feet of the lovely
    lords of might,
They and the courtiers of prudence insured against danger of
    life and number and light.

Forerunners run naked as sharks through water, nose to their
    prey, have message by heart,
Their thighs will be tackled, Look Out, They're away!
    clipping the wind, they've gained on their start.
The wind thrusts knives in their teeth, harrows the stubble of
    parched throats,
The front line licks its fire, leaderless, can they cut their way
    to the boats?
They have never eaten or drunk or slept their fill, and have
    no quick-wit means,
Only envy learnt in feeding the shutfist, pistoned, right
    machines.
Canaille, canaille, what red horizons of anger for humbled
    lives lie
Tumbled up in the old times, the long-fermenting now,
    canaille!
Tradition, if wanted, you can taunt with bequeated pain,
    unslaked hate,
For neither slow-traveling signal from the pyramid builders
    comes too late,
In spite of imposed ignorance. No, nor intelligence from a
    brave new state.

Death, starvation among the corn and coal in banckrupt
    winter,
Bent-rail backs of daily slaves and soiled skin under accosting
    banter
Of flashbabies in back-quarters: where meetings froth loud
    to a rebel note.
Useless. For after smokescreen luxury penitent, cocky
    plebeians trot;

And putrescent tenements breed vermin, tearing holes in
   occasional rags,
Fume from sour mouths of windows, whimper on senile,
   quicksand legs.
Raucous the air and barb-tongued, seasoned with tunes from
   sliteyed bars,
Where, living on credit in blabbing pints, the anger of cities
   boozy stares:
G.P.I., poxed brows: "O, *what the hell! All the duties and
damn all rights!*
*They can't get away with it, they shall pay for it, up to the
neck in it, blast the skites!*

How shall we suffer the little children to come unto us, how
   shall we pay
For the ranged, amorphous faces grey as the creased skies this
   guttering day?
While pushbelly, hunger-currency laymen, cultivating the
   licorice flowers
Of their happy entrails, hand in hand, dance around earth-
   produce pyres
And religious scarecrows navigate with downcast eyes this
   vale of tears?

Already immense shoulders heave edgeways through heavy
   bales of sleep.
Force of confederate, free flangewheels, O runners through
   breakage! give them the slip:
Those with hands like shrinking linen that deprecate the state
   of affairs,
Parsing attitudes, fleas in intricate corridors of interlocking
   hairs,
Those that are Not So Sure that the Poor in Pogrom will not
   be Rather a Bore,
Lips bitter-sweet, they Know by Culture, they know Human
   Nature can Grow no More;
Those that are Game to Grin and Bear it, those that the
   Wear and Tear of, that hesitate
Wagging advice faded and steaming as old maids' clothes
   before the grate,
Those that My Country, that Let us Pray, that Drop by the
   Way, those that are Late . . .

Oh, when damned by the sentence of guns advancing like
ants in tragic line
And stowed away in Death, their own hungry mirror, it will
be fine!

The blood beats drums in the runners' temples, the news is
safe as yacht in cove.
And hearts, throbbing squadrons of nocturnal seaplanes,
moving stars above
Stars fixed in the sea, it will be fine, the ground is cleared,
material stored,
With fervid violence, come, forerunners, release the news at
this anxious port.
Red trains lap the licking rails, east the horizon snarls alarm:
Relief from the wheatfields, printing presses toss their tresses
with steel arms.
Come up! Up up! The thunder at one with your voices in
order chants, things
Are with you, rolling her rump, Earth in bacchantic rumbas
grave swings,
Multiple antennae of blind gunnery tremble, invest the
fibrous night
And the armies' crystal shock makes laughter of girls in a
forest pool out of sight.

Is it true, is it true, have you seen the syllables travel over
lips, have you seen
Beermugs whirled through battered lyrics, children ring
embrace on the green?
Bright women thrown together in laughter, Oh gay,
Oh nothing need anything refuse,
Goldstocking legs in their white foam swinging a country
singing joy of the news?

Joy Joy an unbetweened chorus crowds the air with sound
Burgeoning, they feel surging more loud the birth of well-
being all around
While curveting aeroplanes, leaflets released, toss through
the matador swords of the sun
And the ships cheered by the seminal hail of the captain,
by the people won,

Draw white clothes on, make sure of the sea, open tanned
    arms with love and take
To the long white heather of the waves, a wind of towns in
    cry in wake.

Forerunners with eyes of dangerous landscapes silent among
    the cheering sigh
At the flocks of aeroplanes grazing at stall across the spring
    prairies of the sky.

AFTER FIVE O'CLOCK

A Government official dressed in grey minor
Slipped into a low pub
At the end of the world;
Outside, the rain was falling in millions.

An ancient like a frittered, chalk hill
Monocled the evening paper through a chip of window-pane:
The disgraced words took on dignity.

"Will he tout me for a drink?" feared the Government
    official
Though the ancient stirred no more than thought in a new-
    dead man.

ANNAPOLIS

"No, we can't get a license for liquor, being too near the
    church,"
Said the waiter. The church looked friends enough
On its humble, grassy hillock. So I said: "Excuse me,
I must have a drink." And I rambled on down West Street
To eat and drink at Socrates the Greek's.
On my right the Raw Bar, a truckdriver drinking milk
And a Norwegian second mate glared at their faces

In the mirror. We floated on heat
Like paper boats boys prod in the bathroom.
The white-linen cadets walked with girls of good family
It was the feast-day of the Republic and the girls
In long dresses made a drawing room of the street:
They were like sweet william and buttercups
Like petunia and sweet pea and silver moss,
The haute couture clapped a little askew
On their melodious immaturity.
As I said to the truckdriver: "They are children."
He flashed a sigh and said: "Indeed they are."

Imperceptible darkness plucked its petals
You hear the coloured people's viola laughter
And starlight one never looks up to
Blurs the woollen trees
And the houses with no comment to make. A delicate
      drunk
Weaves his glass limbs together up the street.

The little, red-brick capital,
Its velvet, burgess elms,
Curls back into childhood
Trumphets and tricornes, arteries of fern.
I hold my breath for the expected
According to the mechanics of fairyland.

But then, it is not Hans Andersen, the monuments
Of power lower as in any London. Cadets conduct
Camera-fans to the Governor's Residence
To the Capitol and the Revolutionary General
Leading ghosts on his enthusiastic stone horse.

In the porches, after dinner
Loud-bellied citizens swat flies.
The band blows open the Academy gates
And there a girl-dancer remotely
Flows to the dance.

TANTALUS

The diplomat has bared his head,
The wine spreads across the cloth.
Give me stones for leavened bread?
My spine's pipette will fume in wrath.

I knew a gifted girl, she spoke
Languages more than Noah's beasts,
She took the veil and loathed the yoke,
Flirting despair with Mormon priests.

What will you give me if I tell?
I cannot speak, my hands are tied.
Shame like an Alderman in Hell
Has broke me down till I have cried.

THE BLIND LEADING THE BLIND

Half-hearted, hum low, hide from my
Fool, that my familar is,
Pride slipt on shabby genteel shoe.
Hide the fear and check the spleen.
Lightning like a fever chart
Quickens the last, quick stare at life;
Storm destroys but cunning can
Find crevice there; speak to him, say:
"Be my obedience for a spell
The fugitive causeway fingers sight
Hold your breath like hunting moon
I'll feint with the steering wheel, come
        through."

Storm hunts the moon through heathery skies
The moon at bay reveals her cover
Lights up the windscreen, clears the way
For causeway's clouts of wind and dark;
And my fool fawns on me
His cheek on mine, takes the wheel,
Muzzles my mathematics, his
Nails deaden my temples, breath

And gibber mixed beside my eyes.
Fear melts in the storm, danger
Grows in me till I exult,
Wave the arm, sing and defy
The strapped, consumptive seas beneath.

Every step the first and last
Curlews along their stretch of coast
Rattle their figurative bewares,
Guardian fowl but capped like us,
Cry our number, cry our want!
Hear the measure in my voice.
Sky opens and would take us
With its thirsty light; and we
Proceed above the hooked rocks.

FREEDOM NO OBJECT

Here are empty quaysides
It might be midnight nearby
Or a searchlight stripe on midnight.

Enter, stealthy, who-you-know
Propelled along in torpor
He might be a river flowing
Back to the source, its author

He is pulled up short
By stacks of sacked grain. He
pushes, his legs move
Up and down and free.

CELIBATE RECUSANT

In the jingling, clear air,
Skim over the Temple domes
Birds, those fishes with hair.

Remember the sign fish were
In the incoherent catacombs,
Wombs that gave but mixed birth.

In a tunic, striped and cool,
I lie on the red earth,
Over me kneels my Fool.

Floats from a far shrine
A Virgin, pure of male girth,
The upper air seethes to brine.

She is the first unlike All Them,
Jerusalem! Jerusalem!

She planes down over me,
Endymion and the Moon I see.

"Unclean! Unclean!" my Fool cries,
Hatred of me frees his eyes.

I jerk out what comes next
In the ritual of slaves of slime,
My fear all unstrung:

"Touch me not!" to the unsexed,
Abstract, furious Virgin hung
Above me, time after time

And like a great, dull fish
She floats on: "It's as you wish."

OBSTACLE BASILISK

Down the path through treacherous years blood-dried
My cold-sweat horse, with his incredulous ears,
Ticks off each bandit landmark as we ride,
With friendly snuffling shows he shares my fears.
Those damp rhinoceroses, the mountains, shamble
Past; and hasty clouds tear like bramble
Into its spectral seven the dying light;
The stirrup foot, the reins, renege their lordships,
A mile below is a breastful of warships
In a heroic harbour, menacing, tight.

An old priest's nag pulls up, cries askance
At our disarticulated style:
"Halleluia! Halleluia!" In fractious dance
His legs curve like a weak smile.

Then sundown at the city gates
Defended by a groom and three sick colts
My horse backs away and defecates,
Transformed into a whippet, off he bolts:
I have lived with nobility of emotion,
Thought out my honour, justified my rise:
Is this mean groom my measure? he, my harm?
Shall thus his fear degrade me, slow my arm?
The basilisk, my mercy in his eyes,
Unmans us both; we fade in slow motion
By invisible spider-camera webbed; our cue,
Predestined, robs us of the will to do.

Or could I ever break the servile charm
And gain one step, in scrupulous alarm?

DAPHNE STILLORGAN

The stationmaster is garrulous in
The modest station set in the glen
Bushes wink with brown birdwings
The benches spread their knees, present
Drowsy laps to the sun.
A white cat sacred dangerous within
Egyptian memories considers
Like a marksman a celluloid ball on a water-jet
A tigermoth's fatal rise and fall
On her rank breath.

One shadow makes the whole sky shake
But I flick with instantaneous eyes
The next quick change before the change begins.
The water spouts are dried
Laurel leaves
Shine in the waxen summer.

The clean metronome of horses' feet on the road
Made anguish with clocks and rules which now
Silence beyond measure floods again
Through the trees' green bazaar and patches
Of light like muslin girls in forest lost.
And lost, but after noisy pebble wrinkling
This scene became a pool in air limpid
Restoring to the inimitable Images
Reflections paled but smooth as smooth as smooth.

Fuchsias revive and breathe through scarlet mouths
Rumours on wind
Far-off the humid pounding of a train
Wind-cylinders boom along
Steel wires, the rails drone,
Far-off thudding, trampling, thud
Of thousand pink-soled apes, no humorous family god!
Southward, storm
Smashes the flimsy sky.

Vines, virgins, Guard your red wine
Cross branching arms frail on breasts
Small showers will fall before the rain crowds:
Use them to cool your rind-stiffening flesh
Writhing with blood for sap
To suck the insect-pointed air, the first threat
Of eager ravishers.
Scared faces lifted up
Is the menace bestial or a brusque pleiad
Of gods of fire vagabond?
Quick just in time quick just in time; ah!
Trees in light dryad dresses

Birds (O unreal whitewashed station!)
Compose no more that invisible architecture.

WELCOME MY WORLD

My white tiger bounding in the west!
Only eternal, animal and dumb,
   Give me my merited rest.
The end of Time is when my time is come.

My two arc-lamp globes muttering light
My thorax of wild woodbine offered
    Staid, fiery and slight.
My dark room where voiceless chairs are proferred.

My green dragon from the barbarous east!
Bring the light with ropes of shaken rain
    April swells in yeast,
A baffled virgin with a knocking brain;

The flesh bound in flat, rasping scales,
Reptile, to your fugacity I cling.
    My witch of nursery tales,
My everything, my thou, my everything!

Gannets casually stab the sea.
Each hunting wave envies the next its pleasure,
    Surround me
The spine is blank, body is pure measure.

Marble protectress with vigilant breasts,
His enemy armed against the curious sun,
    Safe in the dark, the chests
May be opened and your treasure won.

My black tortoise from the hatching north!
Geysers and hissing streams, the landlocked sea
    Are back and forth
Beneath the snail and the sleeper with crooked knee.

My olive naiad in Ionian creeks,
My ballad maiden raped in Highland forays,
    World all in fable speaks,
My gun-flanked heroine of detective stories.

Rise and look out the window and dress,
Mother with child, old man with mottled laughter,
    World, be my guest!
And sleep again, go to sleep after

My feast: I'm blind! if oiled athletes preen
Their animal in the glass, if priests refute

Seen with divine unseen,
I'm dumb, my world, without your light, I'm mute.

Return my early my Lisbon rapture, the galleons
Glittered in from Goa rich and mean,
    Immoderate like stallions,
And the sky in chevalier plume-doff of green

And scarlet kept the burghers in suspense:
Glitter and flit, let others envy me,
    Starling, starlet, what pretense
Could any mortal make to let you be?

Dancing with you is dancing with
Water, ashes kindle on my mouth
    To inform you with,
O my red phoenix from the south!

SUMMER JUJUBE

"Give a tip to the chimpanzee on the hanging-bridge."
Bodiless voices will get no change out of me!
The chimpanzee in commissionaire dress
Accepts my Scots coin with disdainful grace.

Dried cliffs hold the blue cove
With brown market-woman arms around
Baskets of fruit. High the cliffs hum
Pinged with voices which a metal bird
Pecks and drops in flat echoes over
Hives in clefts and bee-serviced furze.

And tracing on emphatic, limited scale
Their needle notes, the self-deluded larks
Keep a faint, fixed idea cock-bobbing
In the wanton, berry heads of convent girls
Fretful on the apathetic sand;

Among them one, a bold, a billboard baggage
Like a primping principal boy at the pantomime
Keeps the far-galleried chimp on dancing hoof.

She fires her thighs with hands to learn their office,
Patting her pleasure in her mockeried men.

The Easter vestments of the heat crackle
And egg-backed ladybird and bluebottle,
He of the glossy, royal-blue rump.
Rub sleepy legs without looking.

Now dips her runaway horse, a white sail
Over and down waves of stone ditch,
Rears in invisible lariat, scared
By briary winter sly beneath the bloom.

Her whip exclaims. Horse, to your world return;
Mistress is landmark; friend, the hound
Pouring like milk into his sleep.

Damson on the springboard,
She smiles for the fun of it through orange lips,
Divides the air, the idle water.

POET AND COMIC MUSE

Actress, head tilted, hithering smile,
Advance, advance against me,
Twittering proliferation pruned to style.
Sterilized in us, their passions stare,
Incontrovertible in the floodlit glare.
Come, bunted out in borrowed quips;
You have both enjoyed and incensed me,
We are suspended on the line between our lips.

I am glad no disobedience can
Disarray this axiomatic plan:
The rite
Unrolls with the casual necessity of a bullfight;
Pinned on the euclidean frame
Of the stage, night after night,
Always our sentence and remand the same.

Laugh with your mouth.
On fiction fixed, the general, vague drouth
Is slaked by the neat passion we do:
And winning them I can approach you.

VICTORY OF SAMOTHRACE

Hammers musical round my head, hammers throbbing on the
    roofs
Wary silence of brutal propellors that have suddenly burst
    their speed
All aboard all calling all in all in!
Smell in the rain of mown hay and thistles, old
Red of poppies, creeping warmth of remembered desire.
Heads are markets for anarchic holdings
Are there no shoulders to lean on?
A sweet lady! not alas the invented Lady of Serenity

Fingers of a black-gloved hand tender and vicious on my
    throat
I am snatched up and hurled into the air
sweet lady! on this grey sea you are not preceded by singing
    dolphins, as was Aphrodite
But by discord of winds
Nor by the noise of drums, drums throbbing continuous
    hammers
But are yourself the creator of tornado with your clothes
    whirring about your knees like grouse rising
And your wings
Disturbing the exact harmony of the stars

Victory, winged Victory!

The sea is empty of fish beneath me and there are no ships
Otherwise I should cry for help
But making the best of my own bargain
I offer you as gauges of faith
The beginnings all over again
The never to be forgotten and
The supposed brightness of lamps in daytime

74

Winged Victory of Samothrace!

Let me be always in this state of grace
Keep me going on bribes like this, the unfinished handiwork
    of sunset
Be to me also for a sign
Of burgled outhouses round the inviolable family stone
As a priest uncertain among his mysteries when a bending
    candle flame provokes forbidden images.

A man is swung between two lilies tall as pines. Terror!
Increasing loudness of a thousand feet of men tramping
    down wooden stairs. Throbbing wooden stairs.
I will make another prayer
Give me an object of art, a statuette of Diana
I will caress her limbs closely with my fingers

For these graces, spirit of movement, I will build you
    an altar
To be destroyed immediately
And make offerings of promise
Of heroes once again
Of women's eyes before love has drowned their sweetness
The moment is poised in fear

Our Lady of Victory!

And your voice, which has the opulent contentment of a
    June stream, babbles
And I feel with relief:
Better in danger with the goddess than float like a barge
    on the sea:
Fingers again at my throat

Baptism by immersion in the numerous sea

As the water closes over me, I see
The impersonal gleam in your eyes
And the lax ebb and flow of your breasts.

THE LANCET

Brilliant fierce eagles
And goldfishes asleep.

Lips to drink and instruments for singing
Tight hedgerows gripped the fields, now loose and drowsed.
I moved about in the dark, all was quiet
The skies swollen with unshed thunder
Along the clay path my footsteps
Ominously, softly counted time.

Everyside are spread the fruitful plains
Villages live and die
Beneath the million-citied sap, the indifferent fosterage
Of trees; a bloom of night!
As the bloom of black grapes to your nocturnal sky:
So am I near to freedom.

Now and then a shout floats up
In the court
Where the colleagues
Are drinking and musing. None
Will propose an enigma.

Look straight into my eyes when you drink: Yes;
The same enchantment as ever makes me yours!

Your hair dims
I narrow my eyes to slits and I see
Gold copes gliding
The market places foaming with white smocks
Cantilenas of men and women chained and chanting
Each mouth fabulous
With its proper version.

I have been held back
From acts of particular kindness;
I have skulked in the halls of anger
And with meanness have blighted
The blossom of generous givers

But make it that I tremble
In Babylon choirs, in sonorous congregation
The celebration of belled buildings
And turn by turn stare without terror on
The rapt ravelling and unravelling of tidal generations
In which I am born and give birth and die;
And above that sea
Simple and full the sun.

The drinkers topple over
Come, we are still asleep
Avoid the lunar marshes

Darkness slips
From my face, your voice
Clamours in my blood
The same enchantment as ever!
Your drowsy head,
Dishevelled, falls on my shoulder.
The streams in their beds
Never tire of habit
The same enchantment!
Ebony doors open, my love
Is unfulfilled, yield!
The brothers of the sun, the eagles,
Are fixed among the wavering skies, yield!
Bear fruit of me.

VENUS OF THE SALTY SHELL

Round a cleft in the cliffs to come upon
The Athenians standing with their friendly gods
Serious on the shore.

The fresh violet of the Middle Sea
Blooms and is gone; and there
The tremble of a difference from the foam
Foam forms a shell which bears
The smiling idol of Love
Brightness shadowy through brightness.

The space of a moment love lightens the body
Only when love comes free as air
Like the goddess on the dove-drawn shell
Riding upon the speckled hawthorn waves
Into the rocky ways of the sea-republic.
Look at that hand gently to the breast!
She smiles as if turning all the orchards of summer
Into one brittle petal to touch.

The old men do not remember
The women of their youth,
The young men bend at point like setters.
There is need; she, the desired-with-cries,
Fanned by the ivory air, on the ache of birth
Advances as though her nakedness
Were the first glad woman's for these men

And nearer and the cries of the men
Stop, they are struck still.
The doves, the hawthorn merge in the wrack and
    foam.

EDINBURGH TALE

I love walking with you in the Prince's Street all twinkling
    with strangers' eyes,
The telephone chirrup, the downandouts fit in.
I love your eyelids, leaves landing; armistice settling down
Over a whole wired, limb-laundering province where a
    yellow-hammer
Singing, brings on weak tears;
There is a song from Sean's country
A death aside in the slums,
Your eyes lit up like a theatre.

In the marshland, in moonlight, a hunter drags home.

I love your hands of a drowning man gripping a spar; your
    arms flung wide
Like the forgiving rainbow, and what has been done is
Vain, vain, I love your hands

The shouldered earth
By force lit up and darkened
The rivers through earth's breast

Rose of crystal

And your voice and when you listen:
Arras of the Queen's room in Holyrood
The lute is crisp, the bible voices fervid with scandal,
The lute's notes fall like seeds on the straight, yellow petals
    of your feet.
Rose of June, said the peasants in their ballads
Rose of June!
That Queen, fair body stemmed in cramoisy

Ballads of the donjons jerked up in the brown Lowlands,
Whose mistresses so fine, so rare-ringed,
Secret inside three walls
Kin-blood, their robes of cramoisy:
Alack, had love no luck, old gossip, and lust kill?

The tale ends for having been
No secret after all but the ungovernable, scared birds of the
    heart and the blood risen and the lute like an idiot
I unleash my footpads on your heart
Your heart saying the same word over and over again to
    itself like a happy child.

BETWEEN THE LATE AND EARLY

A drink for a drouth!
What summer have you dried in me,
Holding for taste your body rare?
Give as your mouth
Does, liberal kisses open there
Of all shades like the anemone.

It will be all one
When we tire; but now, ageing suspended,
Loving can stroke day into night.
What have you done

Sweet to my gall? Love, starting light.
Like travel reversed, heavy must end it.

Brighten and be
An amber ounce of June's breath.
Love's favourites are few
Let him have me
And you all instant you all of you!
Nothing willl need us after death.

EVE IN MY LEGEND

The world turns round and leaves the sun.
City fathers, light her way!
Switch on the lights for her! It's done,
For her the town's a Milky Way.
I am near mindless, I could mime
The passions that consume Time.

Today we passed from a yellow street
Into a black one, high and cold
I said to her, I turned it neat,
"Your hair's the sun now, warmth and gold."
The too few suns whose earth, to thrive
Can but in Love's eyes come alive.

Once I had kissed her eyes and seen
My love there made whole by their rays
I knew her better than if we'd been
Together a hundred nights and days
And air whose sunny tongues are birds
Bore with ease our heavy words

As she from my drugged side took life.
I feel like Adam who in sleep
Gave birth to Eve, daughter and wife
Whence his far brood would sow and reap,
Half monster, half philosopher,
Movement by mood conceiving her.

And now stop for a mental spell
The forest-eyed, obsidian After!
Yet let that hundred-headed tell
My arms full of her blond laughter
Nothing to know that is not she
Nor she know anything but me.

WISHES FOR HER

Against Minoan sunlight
Slight-boned head,
Buildings with the thin climb of larks
Trilling off whetstone brilliants,
Slight head, nor petal nor marble
Night-shell
Two, one and separate.

Love in loving, all
A fledgling, hard-billed April,
Soil's gaudy chemistry in fission and fuse.
And she
Lit out of fire and glass
Lightning
The blue flowers of vacant thunder.

In the riverlands
Stained with old battlefields, old armor
In which their child, rust, sighs,
Strangers lost in the courtyard,
I lie awake.
The ice recedes, on black silk
Rocks the seals sway their heads.

No prophet deaths
In the webbed tensions of memory,
No harm
Night lean with hunters.
I wish you well, wish
Tall angels whose rib-freezing
Beauty attend you.

LITTLE ELEGY

I will walk with a lover of wisdom
A smile for Senator Destiny
But I shall gladly listen.

Her beauty was like silence in a cup of water
Decanting all but the dream matter
The figures of reality
Stood about, Dantesque and pitiful.
Can anyone tell me her name?
I will love her again and again
Girl on skis, arrow and bow in one,
Masked in glass, graceful,
Hard as a word in season.

I saw a round, Bavarian goodman
And a Harvard student with a Mohican's lope
Colliding with huge nosegays
Then laughter burst above their flowers:
Absent of mind, they had their wits about them
I laughed at them both outright

And at simpering, peasant statues
Graces and gods would they be!
It was a heady springtime in Munich
Many I knew confided in me
Popu, the champion cyclist
Sigmund, deriding tyrants
And Carlos, who made love shyly
To a furtive, gentle girl
And came to my door, stammering,
"She loves me, you know."
"She loves me, you know."
But geography separated them
And geography keeps them apart
Now they live forgotten in each others heart.

II

The sun was full on, the bird-breed
Gradually found their wings.

The baroque churches glowed like the Book of Kells.
We two, with butterbrot and sweetmilk
Over the snow beneath blue winds
Went far and wide.
Busy, alone, we all go far and wide
Who once listened to each other's
Fair vows and counsel.
Of those that go out of the cafés and gardens
Some lie in prisons
Some die of unhappiness
Indeed, it is so!

This is all I can remember
Quarrelling, gusts of confidence
The class climbing through faun nights
And her I would meet
As though I were unconsious
In vacant, bright-columned streets
And brings in love's tunic scattered to the four winds
For no reason at all
For no reason that I can tell.

PICTURE IN A WINDOW
Les roses sont tantôt passées et les rossignols aussi.
                                                    Racine

Roses are past and nightingales as well.
The mercury streams, this mouse-leaf-moving dell,
Old rusty yards beneath autumnal rain.
Here, in the climate of grief, deciduous bane
Of the faithful heart, the humbled Hercules
Puzzles illiterate accident's decrees;
Here, tired of interlacing, naiads crave
The novel-boned boy and lascivious wave
Moist thighs and hips and stare with mucous eyes,
Untended now their sources rise.
Your finished, angular health their sense enthralls;
Descend, Elysium behind the falls
Grows love-in-Idleness, descend, Hylas,
From the damp impulse of that female mass.

Webs of wet gaslight thread the streets and lanes,
Oily putrescence clots in painted dams
In pavement runnels and in spiderous drains
Which, as my memory, her double, shams
Its blacked-out crystal springs, are flaked with rain
Like scruples in the circumambient brain.
And Hercules fills the offended coffee-stands
With rippling echolalia, his hands
Around wine-cups remember slender hips,
The beachleaves touch his face with waning lips.
The buildings through their thousand windows burn
Saffron in the fog and heads to lilies turn:
O buildings! Wrestling, incandescent tree!
Fewer you burn than want of her in me,
As her smile, leaf-orphan of the streets,
Beckons from mouth to cheating mouth, retreats.

III

No more the inspired hoarding of the fire
In time which most you hate and most desire
(Unless, as sages say, each minute thing,
This beetle and this beetle's broken wing,
Discard their sensual harnessing to rise
A Beatific Buzz in Azure Skies!)
Ah, how, like buds crowded with dew, the skin
Shrank from and craved the listening fingers in
As different loves unite with what they miss!
White moon, white moon, O grant us, Artemis,
Thy gift of lunacy lest bleed afresh
The wound of separation of the flesh;
Lest I relive, mature in swaddling clothes,
That trauma between racket and repose,
Or see in the dark her corndusky hair,
The breath held in, the foot upon the stair.

FAREWELL AND GOOD

She I loved so much will not appear again
Brilliant to my eyes as once she held me, nor
To inhuman eyes in any angel-foaming world.

What use my hermit grief to a world bitten in self,
Bland under omen, but to make more its useless griefs?
Why must, as absence ages, she the more instant cling?

Grief cannot doctor my birthday evil that diminished her
Nor be voucher for recompense of pain at heaven's gates
Nor by crying it for relief do I purge it. Nothing forgets:

Not wisdom teased from the wax and crumble of all flesh,
Powdering between thumb and finger: O wash in moon-milk!
Suck the drug simples in our rock-night scratched by man

In eruptions of mineral continents scruffling to settle down:
Nor though spring lust and shine on the sea and chaffinches
        chatter,
Though light from sunlight down to tombs give me my kind:

Whatever I do, unreal, I may find my hand, once hers,
Bled on the wall in a crack of anger and veins blocked
And eyes glazed that will break open to hers no more;

At any time of the day and night, struck by a wind-flash
In snood of leaves or in phantasms of sleep assembling her
        form,
I restore my kingdom in her, the real that deepened the
        dreamed-on

Ritural loves of legend women admired in childhood:
Then rememberance stings my reason, both entangled in
Grief which webs movement and is merely want.

Still the complaint still no comfort to her and me split
Like a glass, like life split by some Sistine hand,
Our life that brimmed over like diamonds in our light.

LOVE FROM TIME TO TIME

It is the drained head
The mustang tilt of the chin
Farewells hardly count

The passion that was a third life
And we its yoke and white
Has cracked its shell. Can we feel alone?
For the first time I see you clear,
Where is the source of tears?

Day turns over and it is night.
Patient beds, neither wanting nor wanted.
The pouting breasts, the intake of the lap
What are you, dried for want of our sleep?
Let be the thirst, I cannot slake it
The underswell of Time whispers me away.

II

What coasts are these we cling to but the world's
Its walls raised by the frail, learned sight
Which, as they noise down in disaster,
Beguile my ears to thin out the tinkling
Of their most precious panes, wealth and art,
Where are you and I
In the brass flames of our mistress city on fire?

Now courage at love's ending cowers before
Love's transmissions censored in your eyes.
May the whipcord train
Snap and let out from my station! Yet,
O shoulders bent filial
Face in depthless vulcanite washed
From neither's past, from the underlip of the world
Who smile away, now in another mood,
Self-pity and the fear of hardship
Who make love all and neither here nor there:
Still, still, the wound lives beneath the breast.

It's the last barricade, the defenders of the capital
    kill with spades.
Absence is only winter, the valley
Shouldering Nile will flood.
The pointed, clean linen and stiff glass are ready.
After months of familiar darkness
That glinting scarab, the sky, renews the heliacal
Rising of Sirius, daylight
Which does not believe in death.

Lo! Lo! that red, absent drumming!
I have your fingers tight held;
In a few days, the lapse apart
Of our bodies, they, our motor and term.

Nearer than hands as we were
My eyes' membrane went silk with childhood;
Imagine then however one we were
In swift, carnival streets with sanguine flags,
Now your eyes are inert, you are faced away:
Sweet or bitter farewells, it's all a matter.

Love made, there is nothing to thirst for.
Love cymbals the interior hour, the dancer
Fretted out from its blood.

A DREAM OF ORPHEUS

Low and knelt on my knees at the blank bed in moonlight
Listening with sidelong frightened eye to the forms of the
    table
Twitching out of inanimate wood, all from erratic,
Night-risen mineral and plant loose from man's neat
    dominion,
I stroke and stroke the sheets murmuring the old
    endearments:
"Little mouth of honey! thyme breath! lamp of my
    comfort!"
(O Love! sweet protestant soul of pain and guilt and death!

Better be crost and leave like an ignorant avid youngster
Whose gay-plumed brain in dreams dances his body's need.)
But here's a ghost's hand only I hold; and heartsick I think of
Your eyes' Cyprian charm from sacred, ivory centuries,
We lying balanced in night's blue hammock in bright upset
And earnest lark singing so brilliant to faint-come sun
I willed them both in my arms; nor I but the lark called him
Lord of the world, lord! nor I moved, but earth, from sleep.

Now, again, the hour between night and morning softly
Holds city, rock and beast companion in nets of wisp;
Orpheus I am not whose grief sang so melodious, the lion
Shyly drew back his ears, yawned and the sycamore
        dropped its
Branches as now they are; who, powered by magic, descended
Deeper than the pits of guilt to Hell's void, and singing
Conquered back his Eurydice murdered, and Death warned
        him:
"Turn from her yet the terror of human eyes, for death is
Only life's limpness, or she will lapse back with the shades."

Lost Eurydice! beautiful through chance of chance on
        chance . . .
Life, whose indifferent labouring only love can bear with,
Bared to gold-nerved rock: and there rises a pastoral world:
Farmers, serfs of the rain, shrunken wives, goat-smells,
The hunchback wheat to cut, the hunter and his hunger,
Lifelong enemies in that boat blandly sailing to death
(Master from anywhere, comfort them!) all lie, remotely
        harmonious,
In the god's lazy eyes. But in the halt of evening, murder!

Bareness of stone listening, fear and trembling
Take doe pausing with doubled paw, pigeon on half-wing,
And men seeing the forms they knew denatured. Then
        Orpheus,
Priest with power over words, called, so unselfed by pity that
Generosity gave him power over things, called her name:
She with kind hands had wedged the waste in the eternal:
Humbly the hills drew near with shadowy, compassionate
        arms

And as though the dead had suddenly wakened and asked
    for silence,
Silence was; and he murmured, chanted his grief till the beasts,
Nozzle sloped on paw, dimly adored her name and
Lilt-foot fawns nudged bravely up to the quiet wolf-packs
Terrified as all the articulated world trembled apart
At murder's torpid sacrilege: till Orpheus, finder in frenzy,
Sang out the mortal sympathy linking plant, beast and man.

Rise, turn away. And come, O fresh and slim-wind morning!
Love's summer-syllabled arbor ripens to silent autumn.
Rock lessens; creatures grow and fail; the hunter
Ages in the ditch and swallows die on the flight to Egypt.
Triumphant, O sun, hithering from nether voyage to your
    nestlings!
Yet can you not persuade the dead beloved back;
Nor time, with its maganimous saints, counterfeit their vision
So that they walk here perfect before death.
                But Orpheus
Grieves for her still; in the shell and web of her body, beauty
Dreamt the forms his love made substance of and that she
    dreams in him.

VESTIGES
The room dark and tight
As the core of the shut apple,
Starlight none, high up
In the skylight, townlight
Like a tall dahlia
On which smooth eyes in love
Idled for hours long,
Like in a blurred coalpit
A pin-bright vein of quartz
high in the powdery darkness,

Mouth by soundless mouth,
Like subsoil roots
Tense through worms to water.
The unsentried senses
In fenceless pit-shadow

Softly slept on guard.
Moon would have shown the beasts,
Sun the savage men.

But the door sprang to light
And police with torches
Queried the room naked,
The ogling, bogey verdict
Of a tribal justice
Dead sin resurrected . . .
False guilt, false guilt . . .

Nor did the ear hear
The desperate, friendly bells
From the depths of the breast,
With all the world's police
Round the world's love-bed.

LAKESIDE

The wind brushes against my heart.
Lamplight whitens the planetrees, how
Fever is dew upon the elders' brow,
Some may stay together, others apart.
  Breeze blows and the branches sway
  Lovers and beloved gently sleep.

The limpid yacht disdains her crumbling way.
Gods in the sky, now smithies of the Good,
Now iced in astrophysics, heed our mood.
About prophetic dustbins, children play.
  Breeze blows and the branches sway
  Lovers and beloved gently sleep.

Ardou gone miserly in glittering art,
O musty baron above the creeping flood.
Deer fly from the hot, encoaching wood.
The happy and the true are far apart
  Breeze blows and the branches sway
  Lovers and beloved gently sleep.

III
INTERCESSIONS
(1937)

THE ALEMBIC

Heart, beneath monotonous accident
This stillblowing wind springs
No rain no rain enmeshing
Multiple infant feet of aspirant winds:
Least hindrance possible against
Cloistral lashes shut on folded cheeks
Sanction also with a poisoned blessing
Vital examen, for your mining teeth.

Blood's aromatic in my breath, a respite
The wind may unwax my summer, let the
Accountant suspend work, wipe his misty
    glasses
The wind pads almost noiseless like a cat
Do not reject its suave caresses, Heart.

DEATH AND HER BEASTS, IGNOBLE BEASTS

The dried pus of vultures drags the horizon
The noble beasts retired, their turn now, dried
Mouths of my fears are death's vultures craving saliva:
They would feed sick life on the smashed mouths of the
    weak
Whose nostrils death has plugged with stale love-smells
And suicide charms with racked face in a wall of marble,
Their eyes decharged have numbness that looks like peace.

Smeller-out of strangers! curious Death
Your noble beasts were not fearful for they
The emerald bergs of doom, Cybele and the drums,
Startled my stupor into spite at least:
Now your currupt sweet pleading through my friends
Smoothes me like cambric on an infant's flesh
You would enchant with physical dances me
That cannot afford to believe your vultures peacocks.

Unexplained tears suddenly blur my courage
And desert movements in the breast shaking
The forts I built so well already ravaged

By sleep by the cold by the intransigent light
Make your back-alleys seem imperative
There is none so much as you, none you, I think of.

But I turn to move. The antarctic world-specked dream
Grows without sound like flowers, man's bit of air
Throngs deafening ears that could distinguish once
Noises of rivers among the noises of seas:
Yet, Sacker of crumbling towns, I will not agree
To the proposal of peace you made to my friends

Attack me in the dark, I'll extreme fear
With the first of all landscapes given its eyes
In the frantic group of naked man and horse;
With the cheering of shredded men in losts forts
And to go on with, the length of today and tomorrow,
The evidence that lifting needles make the cloth.

WINDTACKER WINDJAMMING

I really don't know what to think
As the wise cat said to the king
When big with proverb
But if it's proper
To get my bearings
At least I'm aware of
My sky changing its costume all day long.

Sometimes a close-eyed steamer outside port
Keeping my eyes about me in these foreign parts
I refuse to budge
Till the pilot takes the bridge
Then in the warm arms of breakwaters pressed
Allow my hold to be cleared without protest:
Which housewife inability
To give without being guaranteed stability
Me more amuses
Unfortunately, than it distresses.

Sometimes a cloudburst of starlings
I take with exaggerated bombardment

94

Of silly chatter trees in Spring
Overwhelming groping speech that needed training.

Rarely when, a clever taxi
With discreet axles
I tow the line without jamming,
My thoughts get such a shock
They set up a most undignified screaming
Like a lot of schoolboy factory horns at one o'clock.

Usually a sea port on the west coast
On my last legs above the rodent sea standing
I doze most of the day to make the most
Of the night with sailors and gin and dance-tunes and candles
Because I know I'm going to totter
Into the sea some day;

And it will be so much the better
If I can slip off gaudily while on the batter
And without annoying the neighbours by piteous bawling
Let's hope I resign from myself gracefully
With no ill-feeling.

LIFFEY BRIDGE

Parade parade
The evening puts on
Her breath-stained jewels
Her shadowy past.

Trailing behind
Tired poses
How they all
Fulfill their station!
The young with masks and
The old with faces
Such an assassin
Such a world!

From the bridge they admire
Their foolish reflection

95

Drowning in birth,
Man's face and centuries
In rivers with stars
Fugitive wheatfields
Giving no harvest...
Here's poulticed peace.
If dreaming of death
Unheavened could but rend them
With anger or envy!

The pigeons creak
On rusty hinges
Turn to the window
Bright with oranges
And girls the girls
The gashed fruit
Of their mouths and smiles
Cute as the rims
Of their cock-eyed hats:

In limp doorways
They try out their heaven
They grind at love
With gritted kisses
Then eyes re-opened
Behold slack flesh
Such an assassin
Such a world!

Same with all the
Young and hopeful
Any relief will
Do for a spell
Then timid masks
Live into faces
Then there is quiet
Desperation

The houses lean
Against the wind
Won't you give over?
Say, what about
That second coming?

Deaf quay walls.
Water wears
The stone away
And out of the river
The arc-lamp rays and the
Wind weave
Try to weave
Something or other
From flight and water.

GRADUAL

Why, how, often, with first the matchlight knocking
  With little alluring jabs, drabness
    Of moist blankets,
Conceding laziness not even got from
  Pleasant defeat in dough splattered
    From arclamps;

In a flamingo of oil-geysers afire once for likeness
  I offered fire to the sun's fire at evening
    On roads westward;
Not even then convinced against exciting
  Metamorphosis, pheasants into beating
    Horses love-abreast;

Last, inevitable executioner, scythes handling
  For every prosperous disorder
    Foresight heartening,
Lighthouse, O regent of the seas trampling
  Jetsam, heady storms absorbing;
    Raper of darkness,

You struck, you tore the cry of the woman that loves most
  Thrown in the straw, warm beast-breath cylinders,
    No farmhands even . . . .
Why, when elect, not fire the retaining bordels?
  Trifler of grace, from surrender shrinking,
    And frenzy of streets.

IN THE LAST RESORT

Me seeing the seen, the prestige of death drives faint,
Coupled asynchronous like time and knowledge.
Lunar scaffolding, a decrepit star falls
Rotting eyelashes fall through fetid wind:
My eyes' tarnished jewels and bright jewels:
Lunar scaffolding bathed in equal light
New starlight reaches earth in safety.

Played as between each other they are grave
Not to be explained by winking of an eyelid
But as against death's cuff on my interrupting
Eyes where the bony earth and iron seas
Knuckle into passion brief and only, then
They are treasure and my affair. And the glittering style
That's named to death because he takes unrest
Comes simply from his being a jewel-thief.

COMMUNICATION FROM THE EIFFEL TOWER

In the court darkness breathes heavily like a woman in labour
Starlight hammers at wary roofs always at bay
Always at bay the houses carry their boatloads of sleepers
Through celestial channels of darkness upset with nightmare
Shying at the shallows of that feeble light, moon, that ally of
    day.

What waitingroom dreariness fades on the bright rose
    wallpapers!
Lamplight drips reluctantly over the windowsill
The air scaly with fish, disgust frictions my skin
Apprehension becomes china eyes become
A wavering plainchant trappist digging his gravesods
One sod per diem, and he stiffens as the vivid sweat
Stings in the roots of his hair.
Shame among the roots of life.
So far for me, turn round
I would roll in the plasmic multiplications of her hands
Convulsive foam on waves which are
Crumbed by cliffs and their reiteration
Stifled at each birth, sucked back

Into the slack marine mass; and she
Fighting for me with any stimulant
Whispers GOBETHAU gesticulates GOBETHAU

That is ill-chosen I have called his bluff
Once from a balcony set at eagle height
He showed me air that first poured brown like glue
And then clotted rigid with human nerves
A saw tore at my forehead

Woman slapped up of ooze, not were you a red angel would
The dreaming whips of your arms into earth absorb me
A close unfabulous animal
Still less his laws you repeat, for as you love me
You take the approximate and safe; but speak ahead
'Whereas' she states 'fortune and misfortune construct
        existence
For the fairer sifting of history
To the more fortunate of our children's children
And whereas it is expedient to have heaven, of dark locality
        doubtless,
Made of distracted eyes the beacon while the hands bought off
In major labour nurse the treasury
Of the minority most virtuous
So, for that this misery of the many is necessary
Avert your countenance while my tribal groups of combat
In a terse putsch strike elsewhere for your sake
Besides our misery's mental, take this girl'
Well no, I must say
And your play of the fatal spy is good at that

GOBINEAU has enpimped you, you have all gone dame
With features and cooing curves as if I had made you
Keep off poisoner of seed pretty flint-flanks
Pivot of a fan of showgirls with a slow lilt to their hips
Will I come? But it is absurd, a bookworm, now, Will I mind
        my business?
Yes I know let me alone your only words are insane.

Let's have breakfast now to pretend it's morning
No, the bell corrodes the silence cover my mouth
Gentle when I am sleeping breathe O summer twilight

The fireflies of your gentle thoughts through my gnarled
    thorntree nerves
Smile through my eyelids soothing as a shaded lamp

Let her not take thee with her eyelids
Let her not bemuse thee with her tongue
All the hawthorn of breasts is comfortless
All the periods of eloquence cannot smother
The mononsyllables of these unwilling unbelievers
Scuffling for a foothold
Prayer choked in their throats
By puffs of irondust of their subsiding works
The prefects of society stare with taut eyes
Try not to hear the exact drumtaps at their ears
The imagined representation of distant barbaric invasions
A snap as of jaws breaking, the windbiffed empire buildings
Crack snap apart, become felled pines
Hesitating into their preying shadows
All the bearers of further tidings dry up such as docked
    ships
All the squadrons of bladed flight
Humiliated, are black beetles so crass in bulk they
Cannot be said to creep but lurch.

GOBINEAU it is why will you keep on saying
    GOBETHAU?
How can you help, you cannot get the words right
Leave me, I'll not be sucked away from memory
Through any fistular brutish throat, how sweet
Brutal and sweet the mouth.

GOBINEAU self-consuming plane
Pure, bitter and sombre as all
Defenders of the past in the obstinate ditches of sleep
Banking on the privileges of age
Which I tell you are no longer honoured
Why mock as weakling the hope of the weak for serene years
Since you'll not be there, why mock, this dog in the
Manger, mangy mastiff, was not once of your masterful
    kindness!
Preside so at this conference of the ancestors
It should be a courtmartial, they have betrayed
It should be courtmartial with death, howso the urbane

Death at bay make smile our eyes with its grace
Because from the wretched their blood avariciously drips
And unheard stealthy as on wool
Famished hordes advance like silent skies.
The lidded anger of the oppressed
Stutters through chinks; and may it detonate!

The seas with lowered heads charge at breakwaters
Wildfire scythes my forest with scythes
And while the baying of rhaphsodic women
March of the maenads bearing torches
Rises through the dissolute fens of my mouth
Gaping in front of surprising hands that drape
With fresh rain and light my turf and my dried bedrock
I hear the humming of my tower
Mounted on guard among the clouds

My tower is far and I have seen it seldom
I know that it is bound in the steel necessity
Of its own girders Time to one end willing
Time which is patience of man and hope of birth.

Unhappiness is easy shed
When an act can be fitted, even at command
As of simple recruits from their knees rising.
GOBINEAU in whom the egoist angels
Again iced our hearts and forced our hand
Into rebellion, beautiful
Disjointed mannequin, pomp is laughter
Just like any Caesar cracked
And you woman of dearth his procuress
Under the pierlamps cold wind and leavetaking and sad eyes
Other side of the gangway always
Cherished nostalgia gone, I am supplied
For needed nourishment with bread and wine
Worldaday my world my life my world

My blood sounds like a scream in the distance
Who then has drugged me?
Moths drag in the walls around my bed
A tall stinking lily turning to fungus
Splits; and the half-stems incline each side
The rotted voluptuousness of half-heads

GOBINEAU you would close me
In a circle of no thoroughfare
I am a bullfighter in this crossroads making passes for life
Among the slipping spears of the arclamps
While the eyes lined up on far benches drifted
Are yellow inhuman wounds

No movement no help alas not any help.
Their suffering looks faked and is not so,
And mine to them, but wrong, we know its cause.
What difficulty in landslides of marble
Stupid irreducible balks my quarrying?
Our opposite provinces in thought are levelled
I would lay my hand frank and quick on your cheek
What nets between make our looks shifty?
Our sin of the same nature and connivance.
And living in the worst of each, we must invest
A third power a mechanic ambassador of our best and most
A leap in the dark from this instant to the next
Living carried to enjoyment over.
Imperious actual, I have no means
Of gathering you away from you
Unless I fall back on my voracious tower.

I might fly from these purlieus of machine forests
White-waxed and festered at the roots by bellowing sperm
I might fly to the Sassanian empire and mould in the margin
Like an old train among the gay weeds of a sidetrack
It will probably be in America this time perhaps Buenos Aires
I dreamt once of Bueros Aires curved
Like a gold worm in its garden of waves of chrysanthemum.

Tower O my subduer Tower my tyrant
Loosen your girders I will become one I will conform
Girders are lovable they are like nubile girls bending
Backwards in arcs asleep when smiles are flush with their lips
Smiles risen goldfish through currents of dreaming, tower
    and pliant
Passed by the ancestors of GOBINEAU
Round the corners in ambush, opium touts
I am by my acceptance reassured
Saying I come! as if a voice asked Will you come?

Exultant with assent, words gay words irresistible
Moving with the Amazon's thunder and the crushed
    humming of its songs its birds
To find its place in the sea, I can find my place.
And now I know my mind I'll sleep it off
I slip on the greased keel of sleep into the cove
Whose water cuffs my temples with plectrum taps.

I am awake pushing streams of water
Over a celludoid slate on a little table
Such as one teaches at, breaks bread, drinks wine
The four horizons are hung with a filmy curtain
It is the figures of men and women
Matrons and seniors, forked and silly maidens
Whose hope or fear death has fooled as life
And the gentle curves of cheek and hip and breast
Distinguished once by the sun have sunk away.
My hands that sweep
The lingering matchflares of the talked-out day
Are looked upon as celebrating bonfires
The dessicated mouths the eyes of reproachful prayers
Hunger and thirst the anger of blood the distress of the heart
Attend and I declaim that I BABEUF
BABEUF and I mixed like the play of the mirrors
Make *table rase* ready for primary needs
Their mouth's tense bows relieve them, releasing fingers
Their eyes bulge like gates opening
Of fortresses at morning full of prisoners
Insisting on promised deliverance

My tower strong swimmer breasts the clouds
Warning me that fruits only follow
Skies anxious with rain and dreary furrows
And before men become dignified
Being not such as light but passes through
By accident like prisms that depend
On a stray hand
But rather their idea operative in them like health
Interluminant with their perfect each:
There has to be give for take although that sweated labour
Make us spit at the pictures of heaven we have painted

At the merchant of honour granting will with sanctions
Therefore let us bare our hold, let us
Offer our passion to the tentacular sadist
There is just one chance we dare not miss this chance.

Even then O Dilatory O You that cease,
In that town where the passages of tenderness
Are so impulsive and so expert
That the charmed inhabitants moving
With the light-sprung southwest wind's annunciation
Provoke milk-drowsy earth to flowers everywhere,
Will untraced echoes not bewilder sound?
And light twitch like the wing of a dying bird?
And why of course your voice, Blood-opiate, speak?
Ah yes and demented tongues grow white
Railing at that piebald natural day
For that its inhabitants fine-limbed and content
Strut in a day blind from its own glare:
Pride of destruction of its secular enemies
Cripples and bickering and web-footed want:
Nevertheless the security of day is precipitous
The world's blatant glare merely hoods us
From dissolute moral violence
And self-sufficiency is evil while
The dead, our true enemies , are silent.

Tower, that snowy steel town though postulant
Of full conscience and its confetti of laughter blown about
In the main street of the sun, then
Summoned when the trestle-blether texts of poverty are
    irrelevant
What can it offer
More than the pretty tinkling of snowy steel?
Anything will dislocate the riveting:
A boy embittered when summer rain smells fresh on hot
    limbs and
Desire trapped in a girl's wet hair breathes
Or a bored mechanic polishing and he mutters
Caught by sight of his face in one of a million rollers
Or the bewilderment of the strong and fair covertly noting
A beloved forehead suave as styles of maize becoming
Restless and stained
Or no news yet from emigrant sons:

For compromise with love defiles youth ever
Content is hollow and vile it will remain
To suffer branding from tools, the senses' servants

Farewell and good to the dead leave us reproached;
And though pain be gone still the unnoticed jungle rain of
    duration patters
With maniac successive steps tramples down;
Anything we know too well or not,
The worm of anguish in the innocent heart,
Anything will startle again that voice
Shrouded in the stone dream of doom
Behind me lies the wife of my tomb, the sea
And in front the land lit up for evening.
Tower that support my view erect
Firm beneath my picture of you, stand
Let BABEUF fade; day not enough but day and night also,
    now night slants
My brothers and my sisters
Shambled through the magdalanian gloom
So near the indifferent beginning that
When night threw up her hair they were her neck
Not long ago, we are fragile, in need of precept.
Tower, graph of the mind and the hand
How the hand has embraced the mind in you!
Graceful result of faith right by a hair's breath
Mounting resolution of awry steel
Be my examplar of the hero
Who grasps his strength with bolts, obeys and only seems to
    sway
When the bad weathers drive.

I am crowded round by the speechless amoeba-night
Massed silkworms nuclear of centuries
Days after and days after tomorrow.
Night my pure identity that breathe
One in all breaths, absorber of all breaths
Night that gestate in symbol-troubled women,
Dumb breeders of being
Wombed in your cathedrals let us watch
Till the forgotten matutinal colours flame
Various the rosewindows through
Tongues of the moon, refresh them in their labour

The stretched and willing mouths of the supple earth
Buttress-arched conceiving in sleep
Teach us the acid experience of the dead
Their different primeval welcome
Persuasive Night
Drug the tigers of desire that prowl at large
That in tranquillity gradual our value flower
Like the young gawky trees
Which they would crush
Night O Clearer than the day
Because the objects of love are visible.

The people look for new commands, uncertain
Like a mother covering her ears
When the last son slams the door and she cowers from its
    echoes
I am made to speak:
'The losses that I count will be unpleasant
On the hither side of light for a long time
Your looks will not leap
The excited escarpments of colour
Nor the broken geometry of shape
You will lend no more to laughter
There will be no grief each for his own grief
But only narrow beds and milk and bread

One thing to comfort us

IN SOME 8 YEARS.

ENTRY OF MULTITUDES INTO AN ETERNAL
MANSION

Each time a hindrance! I storm-inherent
Gripped in the nervous violins of their arms
    Of the Fates of Ignorance
And Solitude milkness
Against whom I strive with these gold legions,

In spite of each failure horrifying our march
In a senseless moment outside heat and cold,
    Behold charming
    That star-crouched mansion:
Come on Come on They'll have to let us pass!

I am thrilled to scorn of the icy slabs of pain:
The Fates like an envious plebs would insulate us but
    What hurts me helps me
    And Fates are invented
Phantoms, nor like tigers carnal vibrant nor cared for.

The lightnings of their hair are whipped out
Open the doors for any love's sake! Open
    To the invading canvas
    Of harbourfulls of hands, the
Darkness resilient is pressed from the slow-lit rooftops.

Conscience at last my scaffolding high in wind!
Be nest of passages for distressed birds
    When I've won nigh you
    We'll be open to nightcomers
From the rarefied clean rain whistling sweetwilled horizons.

Already be glad how with electric look
One weak torchlight, we have cut through
    No more wet limbs
    No handkerchief limp
After regretted mistresses. Smash the windows

How bright our heads laced in blood mantillas!
The price of worth is shame in pain enjoyed
    You seem calm, yet
    Creation, my ferment,
Wounds throb in your nubian flesh, Night!

Primitive days in clouds of fat stank.
O caballeros caballeros hands
    Gnashing with race, fall on
    The gross canaille still stalling
In thoughtless lust the doors to the Common One

Sweetness of blood's vague way across
The bland white plains of operating tables!
  I am well in, loose me
    From these hags these futile
Visions and discourse and the pomp of signs

I demand silence from the arbitrary
That may be ordered what is going to happen
    Crowd work Shock troops
      The first communion!
O clapping hands, desist! the doors fly open.

I V
FIRST POEMS
(1930)

O PALTRY MELANCHOLY

Not of the Magdalen; her body sang with delight
Standing beneath the Cross, her once chapped white
lips red with blood kissed from the feet Christ.
She raised her arms to Him; and her sorrow was speechless
in savage exulation; her sorrow was her salvation.

Not of Orpheus; he made a string and wood
an instrument he plucked and there was music.
Unhappy Eurydice ah! he called,
Eurydice faint down the banks of the river, Eurydice,
unwinding into the subterranean silence
of the dark Oebrian flood.
His sorrow was the silver sorrow of the poets
that bends o'er its own pain embracingly.

Not of Deirdre; she drank voluptuously
the hot and wrathful blood of Naoise, her slain Lord.
Fierce was her sorrow; measured ecstasy
swaying her golden-fleshed body
from warm throat poured the keen.

Not even the sorrow
of the lioness; she has wound over many hills
all the long night: the stars are intimate and cold,
querulous are her whines in the leafy gloom
questions her stolen cubs; at last
she stretches her brown body on the earth
and now and again
her nose moves to right and to left hoping still
to catch a fetid and dear smell on a puff of wind.

O paltry melancholy,
dragging a songless boredom through sunless and stormless
    days
images firing his brain of never accomplished tasks
disarming smile of humility hiding coward delays
on tiptoe in dreams beside action, sophister strutting in masks
of laughter, of child-like pagan of curl-lipped polished doubt,
a timid traveller trailing slow steps about and about
considering which route he shall take at the crossing of ways.

BEFORE LEPANTO: THE TURKISH ADMIRAL SPEAKS TO HIS FLEET

I

O ships!
Before us once again the sullen seas
and clamourousness of winds above her prow
and foam-fleckt stars that pin waves on the brow
of Night in storms; and laggard day that sprawls
where aftermath of sluggard foam
crawls—

II

O many ships!
Great is my grief to call you from your home
of tranquil harbours ringed with flowered quays
and age-pink malls
where white-beard merchants muse in silken ease.

III

Old watch-dogs half-asleep
how as you creep
fumbling your way over the narrow bar
I know O ancient ships
the plumed youngsters swaggering to war
with sunlight dropping from fawn sails, and hulls
populous with wheeling crying gulls.
Then was my hand sure on the tiller, then . . .
O rhythmic swaying scimitar
time was time was . . .
Come, put on youth again
Do you hear, O fleet
a rumour crepitation o'er the sea!
That's Christian cannon crackling. Do you hear

IV

(Sudden my stale sense
vivid with light of Heaven's recompense . . . .
vibrant my ear
with fretted notes that fall

from houris' fingers twanging lutes in the sun
by noise of streams, jasmin-bordered, that run
in miles of murmuring song.
O clarid streams, make musical, make musical
with measured swaying the dusky golden feet
of the blessed four that I shall rest among
answer their voices' sinuous moist call
with sweet
answering. O warm arms, drousy lips.)

V

O westering ships!
This is the last of all
My conflicts, my last salutation
To earth and ocean and their progeny
Therefore let us put on
Brave show with ordered deck and flapping pavilion.

Loaded are we with wiles and victory
Let us go down. We have no hopes or fears,
Fate has kind subtle eyes and life prevails.

Come, brother ships, be comforted, for see
In benediction of your travailed years
The evening spreads fair sunlight on your sails.

ADAM'S HOUSE

This is the house that Adam built . . .
I cannot understand you when you say
That you are praying God because of me,
That I am incense sweetening your way
Smothering your decay with purity.   •

Stinkarum, stankarum, buck . . .

The forest's full of murmurings and streams,
The pool's black wavelets creamed with froth reluce,
Beneath blue numerous leaves cold moonlight streams
On moss-embedded gleaming limbs diffuse

Of sleeping hamadryads mixt with fauns,
Brown Pan yawns, mutters, drops his flute and snores.
The gods are playing on eternal lawns
But kindly mortals sleep on fronded floors.

> *Stinkarum, stankarum, buck,*
> *The old Scholastics say*
> *That the body is filth and muck . . .*

Still you have furtive eyes and coward tears,
Why should you fret the things you cannot know?
Impotent we can but tell the years.
Cover you with my hair; 'tis better so.

> *Stinkarum, stankarum, buck,*
> *The old Scholastics say*
> *that the body is filth and muck*
> *and will be dust one day.*

Pool,
Lilac-fringed, frog-plopping,
Slewthering moist naiads
Among tall fluted reeds.
Cool water, ah freshness
And ah, to a soul parched
Freshness of you, immobile,
Netted in moving shadow
Of waving, silent foliage
And my heart
Not sure of future anguish
Was a linnet singing in branches
To the rain-drop on your lip's corner
To the slumberous glooms in your eyes

> *Riddle-me, riddle-me, rin*
> *Why do skeletons grin?*

The years slipped from my shoulders
Like life from a new-born spirit.
I rose from the dark pit of the putrefaction of the heart,
and of the desolation of the broken will and the
deflected purpose.
The crapulous faces of my evil deeds

Whirled in the fumes of the pit leeringly,
And then dissolved in the sun;
My decay was asperged by your grace,
Immersed in your purity.
This is the term, I said,
To labour and groping pain,
This is the bright-fired hostel
After the tenebrous journey

Riddle-me, riddle-me, rin
Why do skeletons grin?
There is no rest on the journey . . .

O cold voice when you call
Of sirens singing in the morning winds,
And I drew near in worship; and as when
Just men are gathered quiet in a room
And silence slowly throbs with souls; so silence
Impregnate throbbed with consciousness of us.

Your hair was round my eyes
The grisping silence filled
With light notes soft as milk
Of hundred harps and flutes.

Riddle-me, riddle-me, rin
Why do skeletons grin?
There is no rest on the journey.
And death is the wages of sin.

I've had my lesson again; I might have known
Love is no talisman to the mystery.
About my ears the trumpets strong are blown
Of vengeful angels. O the little cry
Of drowning man in the night at the eleventh hour
The lamp is shattered on the perilous tower
That guards the blessed port of Paradise
And round the waste of waters and the skies
Only the carrion flap with whuling cries.

Experience teaches, you know.

NOW

I

The Urn of the Occident is filled
And the blue-flamed serpent is coiled around its base,
And Pallas' bird, fixed in the sepia sky
Moveless as marble, spreads her iris wings.
Patient and proud mirroring of reality;
Arrogant gathering of sense and movement and passion
To interpet to men the profoundest soul of a man
Disgust and tire like a long drawn-out farewell
The Good no longer enfevers the sons of Plato,
Pure white and azure sky
The Hymn to Beauty is no longer chanted
Dull cold and ivory Aphrodite.

II

Eternally emerald pastures of Ireland; English lanes winding
One-ery, two-ery.
Through smothering blossom; old book shops in Paris;
Ziccary zan
Larks singing in Sussex and Deirdre's now bloodless lips.
Hollow-bone, crack-a-bone.
Vines in Avignon rich-smell charged, and brown men of
Connaught.
Ninery-ten.
Honour redeemed through war; humanity's progress
Spittery-spot.
Sweet things of home; Wanderlust tightening the throat.
Eleveny-twelve.
White hands like peace of the woman who loves me, warm
palm of my friend,
Tweedle dum, twaddle dum.
O Bridges, O Belloc, O Blunden, O Chesterton, Yeats,
O La Mare!
Diggery-delve.

III

Oner-ery, Twoeery
Ziccary zan . . .

116

Let us be Anarchists by all means
                How many miles is it
Dethrone the Verb and the Substantive
                To Babylon.
Roses do not smell sweeter than beans
                Babylon.
Hail to the Holy Adjective!
                Three-score and ten.
What's beauty, truth, life, love, what's me?
                Can we get there?

Don't know, don't know, don't know.
                By candle-light?
Pull down that gilded rubbish. We
                Candle-light.
In metaphysic, apotheo-
                How many miles is it?
-sise Adjective. Hail Sitwell. We
                How many?
Feed on our own decrease.

                Can we get there . . .
                One-ery, two-ery
                Ziccary zan . . .

IV

The Urn of the Occident is filled
And waits for the Embalmer.
The Blue-flamed serpent is coiled around its base,
And Pallas' bird, fixed in the sepia sky
Moveless as marble, spreads her iris wings.
The Green moon and the mauve sun dead in the sepia sky
And the orange grass attend the Embalmer.
Let him come, smooth-paced, urbane

Let him impose resigned hands on these rich ashes
Of the Tuscans and of the Castilians
Of Weimar
Of England and of France
All is here in these rich-smelling ashes
And when the Embalmer, vague, decadent

Such hands shall have imposed,
Let him go.
His eyes are of desolation,
How many miles is it?
Like a cat's eyes in the dark window of a lighted chamber.
To Babylon.
The world is sudden a medium grey; and he beholds
Can we get there . . . ?
Quick hypnotised, the wooden hobby horses
Roundabout roundabout roundabout round
Roundabout roundabout roundabout round.

Can we get there . . .
One-ery, two-ery,
Ziccary . . .
Roundabout roundabout roundabout . . . .

V
POEMS PUBLISHED POSTHUMOUSLY
(1963)

JEALOUSY

Most & most dear & near, though seas divide us
Yet their improbable linking joins us mine;
Your oracles have been my thought in the mine
Sleeping alert, like earth to the moon confided.

Time can have hurt & suffered, served & chided
You, and you still endure intact, O fine
Head held in a bowl of air, no sign
Is needed, each other's beside us

By flesh & seas with their trade-routes enraged
Through which leagues-long, how tortuous straights &
    bends
Space is yet corporal & safe, and so why care

If the heart's pulled askew by alien ends:
We have each other like a wild beast caged
Whom momentary tourists would tease but not dare.

AZTEC IDOL

The Dolls of Revolution, the old-world Faith
With All Souls flow reluctant back to death;
The air's too thin for a rational man to tell
Where Heaven hinders him not, or helps him Hell.

Kind North atheists here who never have known
The God that turned on nature, and was gone,
Admire in the museum the sculptured spite
With which the brutal Aztecs fouled their sight—

The wormy lips, the blood, the useless eyes,
If we look long, we're stupid like scared ewes—
Even Maximilian and Fray Juan have lost
Fear of the future, horror of the past.

This singing child, O I wish she could dance away
The sick voices that never can say their say,
Dancing for the sun, that hidden yellow bird
Singing away in the dark with no saving word.

VAL D'AOSTA

"Yes, yes, I said I was wrong" the curé muttered.
Out front, the mountain rode into the sky
Lifting his clouds, his daughters riding high.
Below, the boyish, red Ferrari sputtered.

"Yes, the children now wear thick ski-boots
But when I was young, father made mine out of wood;
Now, like little lawyers, they temporise to school
With brief-case, and dressed up snug in fur-lined suits".

The Ferrari backs, then moves into forward gear,
In a moment will lie like a rose petal on the mountain.
From Milan and Turin, the Vespas spread like a fountain
The peasants' dream—What will happen is all too clear.

My poor Father Jacques" I said "but what can you
    do?
If the children can buy the balloons with pennies from
    mother—
Thank the Milan millionaire; and drink up, have another
Even if your beautiful mountain itches all through".

"Yes, yes my son! but surely I may remember,
Before the publicity man embellished our beauty,
The dialect was the one shirt for pleasure and duty,
Its Word was rock and river, pine-breath and ember;

We've got to learn these tongues, their tenses and moods,
French for our culture, Tuscan for our trade;
But when the mountain listens to hear what I've said
It's in my language he listens, and rides with his clouds,
His trout puffing boldly up into animal air,
His river talking to itself, his fox in the lair".

MOTHER SUPERIOR IN THE CITY OF MEXICO

It was the tone of grief that filled their voices, not grief
    itself, these children, because it is impossible to forget.
Because of all lands, like the Leinster I came from, where the
    mist blurs the blue country flowers,

This is the yellow and Spaniard black, where the brain
    approaches love and the heart thinks,
This is the land where life and death are separate.

Small birds and small children live apart
    where death lives and where life dies,
Pioneers, my children, lamenting all the same, Czech farm or
    Prussian manor,
O my land of death was Denmark, let us Sic or Sic,
The blue haze in Northern woman's eyes and the crash of
    Italian roses!

Let us say, and Connaught too, O small Catholics, small
    Aztecs, the cloister is quiet where the horses came.
And I don't think it's any better, the stupid Spanish
    Catholics hurting this race, or the low Cromwellians
    failing to hurt my race
Because Man was murdered for God's sake, just as God for
    Man's sake, and
These Indios butchered by bound-brain Spanish Catholics as
    were my gentle ancestors by bound-brain English
    Protestants:
Forgive and forget, they say; better forgive than forget,
    better forget than forgive . . .
And who am I, or anyone, to assume the vengeance of
    my race?

Or any race? Because the proud and the humble both breed
    vice.
My neighbour, with wild eyes and stupid hat, he says, the
    bulls of Mexico burlier than in Spain, the honour of
    bulls more honourable here, the National sport, the
    national guttersnipe in the gunnels, the gripe; but all I
    see is
The bull; all I see is the greedy ringworm of death on that
    noble black head.
Better paid than in Spain, the killer: and more degraded in
    style, I hear, facing the beast, the cataclysmic beast
    all eyes,
The handkerchief of Spanish honour more contemptible . . .

Aztec and Spaniard, proud and surly, proud and separate.
And both gabble about their furious ancestors. And savage

the same bull and the same human heart. And civilise in
Soccer and beer.

Both their fathers, Don Pedro and Quetzalcoatl, who is
almost Don (but I leave out the Lady the Dons brought
here and the dark Mother who couched these Indios:
Our Lady of Guadalupe!). Here come Canadians from
the barbarian ice and Argentines from the barbarian
pampas . . .

When the Dons came, there were no horses here, Don Juan
nor Don Quixote have no place in this land without
ghosts. Where the Atlantic falls tepid and timid on the
left in Vera Cruz and the long Pacific on the right
climbs dangerously, without ships, into Acapulco . . .

There is a small irrelevant boy, scuffing with his thumb
in the dust: "Madre de Dios"

Because it is impossible to forget, Let us say I whisper to him
the last things from the Old World, a poor thing to
that thin-shouldered carnality, terrified between

Voices from the vulpine Atlantic and wolf Pacific jaws.

ABEL

Who was it loved me in the Bible times?
It was my brother, best of Father's brood.
He led me through the hot, inhuman wood
And told me tales of our far Father's crimes.

I in the rear, the other in the van:
Until he found out murder for the better;
I learnt the law, the spirit and the letter
The handcuffs and the flail, the fall of man:

Until the bright seed burst! And world was waste;
My Father, wretched, blamed my brother Cain
Who cried: "The world is waste, the world is vain,
Bloodshed and seed, how bitter to the taste!"

124

3
UNPUBLISHED POEMS

HOBBY-HORSES

Decorated circle, mesmeriser!
Lifeless procession prompted by the child
Astride his wooden horse that plays up well
With silent snort and fine, detached tail.
They say the gaudiest emperor when he tops
The Caucasus of his ambition, feels
The vacuum of his ambition again,
And any John-Joe in his pipe and slippers,
Startled, may see his mind, caparisoned
With a menagerie of wishes in full, cacophonous cry
Sparkling around a tame ring of wire.
Good hunting, side by side, tiger and jackass!
Never grieve, child, flaunt your sword-arm,
Your dauntless blond hair.

PICCADILLY CENTRE

In sun-shadow, I lock away
The files, blue and buff,
Each with a whole life trembling on the lip,
The public clock snapped in light.

I said: "The peaches will fall".
The brick wall in the County Dublin garden
Was drowned in their silk maturity.

Where, by a wall standing up straight,
In summer, sunk through its superficial
Leaf and solemn cattle, does there stand,
Hand on breast, eternal woman
Waiting with half-awakened lip?
Echo of birdsong having ceased.

BY THE BOAT TRAIN

The green flag waves,
The platform glides away, the pillars, the other trains
And that young girl cherished
The space of a smile on foreign passed-by lips.

I breathe new air,
Released from her candid empire.

But if it is so free and pleasant, why
Must I imagine tears and unclasped hair,
And her alone with only sleep to caress
Her spent eyes?

POEM

Waking in her arms of brightness
I feel as natural and safe
As children in their mother world.
The window brightens like a face
As morning opens the sea to the liners
And unparcels the cold towns.

Let me invent. I, day with eyes,
Am master of her, mere invert night;
Those eyelids dam the hundredweight
Sluices of light: she does not know:
And conscious I am king-priest
Of the mystery I have and watch.

Yet she is free, asleep and awake.
The bird's sharp note changes her face
Penetrating to her dream
Shut behind the impregnable
Petal walls of eyelids sweet,
Though I cup her face with fearful hands.

So precious that I realise
How it would be if she were not,
Because embossed upon extinction,
Burning and shining like the sun.
And from that black enemy, sleep,
May she emerge gold and shining!

128

TIGER-EMPEROR

The emperor who thought he was a tiger
Had kimonos with black and yellow stripes
He would pounce on his Lord Chamberlain

His shoulders are broad as a water-carrier
His head small and buoyant like a bluebell
Handsome and eager as a racehorse.

But, pity's me! The Emperor's tremulous voice!
(Only a few subjects know it)
The voice peters out in a shameful treble

There was no Lord nor Guardian in that mouth
He could not manage his million universes
He stayed dumb; the Chancellor wept often.

The Emperor walking up and down, ceaseless
Before his vast, cloudy mirror.

GOOD-BYE AND GOOD LUCK

Here are the world and his wife
Dancing, freed in a frame;
And you, a slow lilt in my arms,
Wrap us in conscienceless life
Where, decorative, harmless, flame
Gold war, black towns, red farms.

If we weaken and go love's way
We'll have no more to choose
But live in the rut in distress
As most men do; and no play
Can this neutral freedom excuse
If our life or life profit less.

Come, darling, a kiss for away!
Now under our thoughts and our hide
Trim Tyranny glides full speed;

It would be mean to delay
While others pay life for our pride,
Strong lads with their useless seed.

Blood without horror shed,
The incredulous womb in dearth,
The faun discharged by his year
Spits on the wine and the bread.
Oh, give back her salt to the earth,
Then we may love without fear!

BOYHOOD

It was a sunny morning
And we were truant both
I spent my only sixpenny piece
And she was nothing loth.

The skiff was light and lissome
My girl was light and gay
I paid the fare, I took the oars
It was a bright Spring day.

All day I rowed that river
Bold of brain and brawn
Looking with longing upon that lissome
Body the sun shone on.

I did not know her countrymen
Had lost their sister dear
We had eaten and drunk, and we rested
Above the sucking weir.

Oh, they were savage gentlemen
Kneeling on one knee
They laughed while the skiff sank in the river
And the river sank in the sea.

RENEWAL BY HER ELEMENT

The hawthorn morning moving
Above the battlements,
Breast from breast of lover
Tears, reminds of difference
And body's raggedness.

Immune from resolution
Into common clay
Because I have not known you;
Self-content as birdsong
Scornful at night-breakage
You seem to me. I am
Fresh from a long absence.

O suave through surf lifting
My smile upon your mouth;
Limbs according to rhythm
Separating, closing;
Scarcely using my name,
Traveller through troubling gestures,
Only for rare embraces
Of prepared texture.
Your lips amused harden
My arms round you defiant,
You shirk my enwreathing
Language, and you smile,
Turning aside my hand
Through our breath's light leafage,
Preferring yourself reflected
In my body to me,
Preferring my image of you
To you whom I achieved.

Noise is curbed attentive,
The sea hangs on your lips:
What could I do less?

It is over now but once
Our fees were nothing more,
Each for use of the other
In mortgage, than a glance.

I knew the secret movements
Of the blood under your throat
And when we lay love-proven
Whispering legends to sleep
Braceleted in embrace
Your hands pouring on me
Fresh water of their caresses,
Breasts, nests of my tenderness,
All night was laced with praise.

Now my image faded
In the lucid fields
Of your eyes. Never again
Surprise for years, years.

My landscape is grey rain
Aslant on bent seas.